THE BIG WE

The Big WE

HOW GIVING CIRCLES UNLOCK GENEROSITY, STRENGTHEN COMMUNITY, AND MAKE CHANGE

HALI LEE

SWEET JULY BOOKS
A zando IMPRINT

Zando supports the right to free expression and the value of copyright. The purpose of copyright is to encourage writers and artists to produce the creative works that enrich our culture. Thank you for buying an authorized edition of this book and for complying with copyright laws by not reproducing, scanning, uploading, or distributing this book or any part of it without permission. If you would like permission to use material from the book (other than for brief quotations embodied in reviews), please contact connect@zandoprojects.com.

Sweet July Books is an imprint of Zando.

zandoprojects.com

First Edition: March 2025

Design by Neuwirth & Associates, Inc.
Cover design by Christopher Brian King

The publisher does not have control over and is not responsible for author or other third-party websites (or their content).

Library of Congress Control Number: 2024949152

978-1-63893-151-5 (Hardcover)
978-1-63893-152-2 (ebook)

10 9 8 7 6 5 4 3 2 1
Manufactured in the United States of America

• CONTENTS •

Part III

Imagine millions of people meeting in thousands of living rooms, book groups, and high school gymnasiums from Omaha to Ocala, from Birmingham to Bellevue, from Freeport to Fresno. We meet to figure out how to fix broken traffic lights or address playground repairs. We discuss wheelchair access in the local park, school board elections, or the next block party. We eat, drink, laugh, and argue together. These simple activities, however mundane, are in fact the building blocks of civic engagement. Simply put, civic engagement is when people come together to improve their communities or address social issues. It is joining forces to do good. It is people who care, exercising their citizenry muscles to make positive change with one another.

At a sociopolitical moment in which there is so much loneliness, isolation, distrust, and disenfranchisement, assembling with friends, neighbors, and colleagues to improve our neighborhoods is one way we can begin to reknit the ties that bind us. By circling up in fun, convivial, neighborly ways to make our towns fairer, freer, and more open for all, we can practice civic engagement with one another. And if ever there were a time to do that, it is now.

Welcome to The Big We.

The Big We is a group of high school students who raise money and decide, together, how to support their local charities. The Big We is a group of women sitting around a living room, raising resources to elect state legislators. The Big We is a group of friends and neighbors who pool their time, resources, knowledge, and empathy to fund community organizing in Brooklyn. The Big We is a book group who pools money at their monthly get-togethers so they can give together, based on some shared values. The Big We is a group of work colleagues who collect $20 every pay period to fund emergent issues in the neighborhood.

The Big We is all of us, in church basements and around kitchen tables across the country, doing what we have always done for as long as we humans have lived in communities—banded together and joined resources, to help one another.

Our American democratic system works only when its citizens—that would be us—are civically engaged. This book is about philanthropy, the sector in which I work, but it's also an American story about how we can be better citizens. I've been working in the social change and philanthropy sectors for over twenty years and have seen the work from multiple angles. As an executive director of several nonprofits, I've sought grant funding from foundations and philanthropists (also called donors). As a board member of the New York Women's Foundation, I got to participate in the grants allocations process. I've seen firsthand that philanthropy is way more than money, especially when it is practiced in groups, because in addition to money, most of us also volunteer our time, lend our influence, and use our voice to bring about the change we want to see. Groups of people who give together are known as giving circles.

I started the Asian Women Giving Circle eighteen years ago with ten girlfriends. To date, we've raised and distributed

$1.5 million to Asian American women and gender-expansive folks in New York City who use the tools of arts and culture to bring more joy, fairness, opportunity, and equitable social change to their communities. I also cofounded the Donors of Color Network, the country's first-ever community of wealthy folks of color. And I helped build Philanthropy Together, the first-ever philanthropic infrastructure organization built to support collective giving and giving circles globally.

THE ASIAN WOMEN GIVING CIRCLE, the Donors of Color Network, and Philanthropy Together are all examples of The Big We: people coming together to be more powerful than the sum of their parts. The Big We is, in some ways, a critique of billionaire-led, technocratic philanthropy, but I hope it also embodies some ideas for those of us who care about civility, community, and taking care of each other.

At its core, The Big We is about generosity, bigheartedness, its joys, and its laments. And it's about belonging. There's something very "us" in the continual striving, the aspiring, the struggle to find belonging with neighbors and friends. This is an American story, but I walk around the edges of it. And like many such stories and ideals, this one is aspirational, in progress, full of grappling, and also some heartache.

Diversifying and democratizing the field and practice of philanthropy has been a goal in my work. Seeing myself, a Midwesterner with Korean roots, in the American story has been a core part of that. And building philanthropic projects so other people of color can see themselves in the philanthropic story, so I can see myself in the philanthropic story, has become an important throughline.

I grew up in Kansas City in the 1970s and '80s. My brother Eli and I were the only Asian kids at our elementary school until Kim Wang came in fifth grade. Kim and I are friends to this day. Eli and I were good at school and athletic and always had lots of friends. When we were in first and second grades, two enormous sixth-grade boys chased us home from school, yelling and taunting us, "Chinese, Japanese, dirty knees," making their eyes slant up, and telling us to go back to where we came from. Sure we were going to die, we ran into our house. The hero of this story is my mom. She chased down one of the boys, marched him into our kitchen, and made him call his mom to tell her what he'd done. By this point, he was a blubbering, crying, sweaty mess. She called the school principal, Mr. Dill, too. Another time, when we were visiting my grandmother in Chicago, a very scary older white lady on the bus told us to go to the back of the bus where we belonged so she could have our seat. The bus driver stopped the bus and told the lady to get off. Another time, in ninth grade, a group of white girls painted swastikas on the lockers of some Jewish students and spewed hateful rhetoric at the small group of Asian and Black girls who attended our school. About once a year throughout my childhood, something awful happened that had to do with race, belonging, and othering. Fast-forward to now. Paul Brest, a giant of the legal and philanthropy fields, practically apoplectic that I was disagreeing with him at a small philanthropy gathering, said to me, "Well, Hali, maybe you don't belong in this room."

Belonging, or not, is a recurring theme in the experiment that is America. The debate over who belongs in this country is very much alive today. And yet the beautiful, hard truth is that belonging is an ideal that we can create only if we do it together.

The tension over who belongs where can be seen in many fields, including philanthropy. When I started the Asian Women Giving Circle, we were excluded from philanthropic networks because giving circles, groups of people who pool their resources and give together, were not considered proper philanthropy. When we started the Donors of Color Network, there were literally no philanthropic homes for wealthy people of color because the existing donor networks had failed to meaningfully integrate themselves to include people who were different from their founders.

Philanthropy, as a professional field and sector, was born out of America's first gilded age. In the late nineteenth and early twentieth centuries, individuals like Andrew Carnegie, Cornelius Vanderbilt, John D. Rockefeller, and Henry Ford made unimaginably vast fortunes in the steel, oil, railroad, communications, and automobiles industries. These titans of industry donated enormous sums of money to create perpetually endowed philanthropic foundations from which modern philanthropic practice and grantmaking emerged. They were aided and abetted by changes in laws and tax codes that privileged the accumulation of wealth and charitable dollars being sequestered this way.

We are living in a second American gilded age, with recent fortunes made in finance, retail, and technology powering our era's philanthropy. Think of Bill Gates, Melinda French Gates, Mark Zuckerberg, Elon Musk (except Elon Musk is not all that philanthropic), Jeff Bezos (and his ex-wife MacKenzie Scott who is way more philanthropic than Jeff), and the Walton family (who own Walmart). As during the first gilded age, the gap between the haves and have-nots has grown ever wider, and we have seen a concomitant explosion of billionaire-powered philanthropy.

Today's billionaire philanthropist tends to apply business-minded ideas and structures to his philanthropic practice. This makes sense because often he made his money as an entrepreneur. This style of philanthropy is called strategic or technocratic philanthropy, and it has been the dominant model for the past twenty years. Metrics and evaluation are key drivers of this model. In short, strategic philanthropy is grantmaking that applies business models, tenets, and practices to the social sector to improve the odds of achieving results by focusing relentlessly on goals, evidence, and outcomes.[1] In technocratic philanthropy, the wealthy donor is the subject and central figure, the sun around which everything else radiates.

You'll note that I've used "he" in this section and that's intentional. While there are lots of women and even a few nonbinary people involved in the running of these foundations, they are almost always organized around the influence of the progenitor, the original wealth holder, who is often Mr. Rich Guy. For shorthand in this book, I will call this big-dollar, billionaire-powered, donor-is-sun-king, individualistic, strategic, technocratic form of philanthropy Big Phil.

THE BIG WE is the polar opposite of Big Phil. The Big We is bottoms-up while Big Phil is top-down. The Big We is often anonymous, while Big Phil is almost always attached to a big name or corporation. The Big We is a giving circle that sits in comfy chairs around a living room or perhaps around a kitchen table. Big Phil sits at the head of a rectangular boardroom table, gavel in one hand, *Robert's Rules of Order* in the other. The Big We is a people-powered form of giving and being civically engaged. The Big We exists alongside Big Phil and, in fact, and of course, precedes him by millennia. Humans have been practicing "philan-thropy" far before any gilded age, before the word *philanthropy* even existed.

To begin to understand the Big We, you have only to look to the traditions of giving in your own families and cultures.

When my family immigrated from Korea in the late 1960s, they were part of an early wave of Koreans coming to America after the Immigration and Nationality Act of 1965, which put an end to long-standing quotas that had favored arrivals from western European countries. My parents and grandparents had survived a hundred years of brutal colonialism and cultural erasure by Imperial Japan. They endured two horrific wars—World War II followed only five years later by the Korean War that divided our tiny country into a North and a South. My maternal grandfather, Chi Chin Hahn, was imprisoned, tortured, and nearly killed by the Imperial Japanese Army for his sin of being a scholar and a freedom fighter. A few years later, he was force-marched by what became the North Korean army and never heard from again, leaving my grandmother alone with six children including my mom. Growing up, I heard lots of stories about scarcity, loss, and surviving with very little. But I also heard so many stories of radical abundance and generosity.

LIKE MANY KOREANS who survived that time, my mother's family were refugees in the southernmost point of the Korean peninsula. They managed to help and be helped by those around them. My mom remembers getting clothes from Baptist missionaries. They lived in one room that was given to them by a distant relative, in a shared house with other refugee families. Later, after people were allowed to return to Seoul, my mother's family found their home severely damaged by bombs and emptied of all their furniture. Yet it was their home, and others who were even more displaced came to live with them. One by one, my grandmother sent her kids to the United States, often via university and church scholarship programs. Eventually, she helped other young people who had lost their families come here, too, including a North Korean orphan, Dr. Do Won Hahn, who ended up working at Johnson & Johnson and was part of the team that developed the birth control pill.

As these early Korean immigrants arrived in the United States, they brought many cultural traditions that persisted in spite of the enormous differences between their new homes and the places from where they had come. In the 1960s, there were no H Marts, so they made *jjajangmyeon* with spaghetti and Campbell's beef barley soup. They concocted *kimchi* from cucumbers, scallions, and paprika. They celebrated Korean holidays and milestones—Chuseok (harvest festival), a baby's first one hundred days, *hwan gap* (sixtieth birthdays), and Lunar New Year—with the food and accoutrements locally available. In the cases of my mom, dad, aunties, and uncles, this meant Morgantown, Virginia; Los Angeles, California; Northampton, Massachusetts; Lawrence, Kansas; Albuquerque, New Mexico; Silver Spring, Maryland; Storrs, Connecticut; and Owensboro, Kentucky.

Another tradition that made its way from Korea to the United States was the idea of a *geh*, or a shared saving circle. Who knows where *gehs* originated, but it was usually women who ran them because they were excluded from the formal economy, including banking. *Gehs* became popular after the Korean War when people needed money to start businesses or for weddings and other familial events. Regular people could not borrow from banks during the war years, so they had to rely on family members, unscrupulous money lenders, or *gehs* in order to raise cash. In Kansas City, my parents were in several social *gehs* when I was a kid. The *geh* might meet monthly, and every member (or couple) might put $100 into the common pot. Let's say there are ten people in the *geh*. Each month, one member takes the pot home—$1,000! The members take turns taking the pot home until the cycle is complete.

I've been part of a few *gehs* with my girlfriends. My friend Shinhee was usually the instigator. Ours was a social, rather frivolous, and always raucous *geh*. We would meet once a month for lunch, often at a ramen place called Ippudo because it is delicious and not too expensive, to pool our earnings and pass them off to that month's recipient. There were usually four or five of us, putting in between $200 and $400 per month, depending on how rich we felt. That made the pot anywhere between $800 and $2,000 per month! Min Jin often bought herself a beautiful piece of jewelry. Sang once bought a gorgeous handbag. Shinhee bought a couch. One time I used mine to buy a new laptop; another time, a stupidly expensive set of dishes I had been coveting; and another time, to throw my husband a birthday party. You could use the money any way you wanted, but you had to show and tell the next time.[2]

Gehs work because they're built on trust, friendship, and shared cultural heritage. Trust is important because if someone leaves midcycle, that diminishes the pot for the people who come next. Sure, it's possible to cheat the system, but for the most part, people don't. I've heard of giant *gehs* in Queens, New York, where the pot might be a quarter million dollars. A member might have to wait five or ten years for her turn, but with an "under the mattress" amount like that, she might start her own business, put a down payment on a home, or send a child off to college.

And while *gehs* aren't necessarily philanthropic in nature—there was nothing charitable about our gorgeous dishes, couches, or jewelry—they are linked to attitudes around sharing resources and communal care that translate very naturally into something like a giving circle. My family were immigrants and had lived through two wars. Money was, by necessity and by its very nature, a matter of survival and a resource to be shared with an expansive definition of who is family.

It turns out that *gehs*—or something like them—exist in most every culture. They're called *tandas* in Mexico, *sou sous* in parts of Western Africa, *i-sou-sous* in parts of the Caribbean, *sòls* in Haiti, *tam tams* in Vietnam, *mahibers* or *ekub* in Ethiopia/Eritrea, and *arisans* in Indonesia. Folks of Jewish faith have *tzedakah*. Muslims practice *zakat*. Christians practice tithing. *Dāna*, the practice of cultivating generosity, is a concept shared by Buddhists, Hindus, Jains, and Sikhs. All of us have inherited cultural practices around generosity, giving, saving, and sharing, but in recent years, many of us have moved away from these community-oriented approaches.

Despite these deep roots of generosity, we find ourselves in a moment where philanthropic practice is bogged down in bureaucracy, strategy, and logistics. Too much of giving has become technocratic, transactional, and skewed toward the super wealthy. Which means too much of philanthropy's bounty has become constipated, stuck within the gears of bureaucratic forms, funds, and logic models. How can we unstick that wealth and help it flow as it was meant to do? How can we move from the mostly transactional to something that is more transformative?

The Greek root of *philanthropy* is *philos*—love. This is what philanthropy is supposed to be about: love, not logic models, strategic plans, theories of change, or billionaire tax breaks.

While the America that we know today is elbow-deep in tax codes and paperwork, it's worth remembering that this has always been a land where we've held space for generosity and communal thinking. Back in the first half of the nineteenth century, Alexis de Tocqueville wrote about the American "art of joining." He made the case that free and active associations are a necessary part of a functioning democracy, noting that "when necessary, [Americans] almost never fail to lend one another a helping hand."[3]

Of course, by the time de Tocqueville was studying and writing about America, there were millennia of existing Indigenous practices of mutual aid, generosity, and community support. Add into the mix the cultural, spiritual, and mutual aid practices of enslaved and free Africans, and their struggles for resistance, betterment, and freedom. Immigrants, refugees, and seekers of a new life—people from all over the world have added their cultural, religious, communitarian, and giving practices into what we now call American philanthropic practice.

So how can we get back to the roots of our own cultures of giving and generosity today?

Giving circles.

While giving circles might be an unfamiliar concept to many, the practice of getting together and pooling resources is part of our cultural endowments, and in the pages to come, I hope to show exactly how we can draw on the traditions of the past to make way for a more generous, more civically engaged future.

Giving circles are simply people coming together around common purpose and shared values in order to do good for their communities. And importantly, giving circle members use pooled resources, namely money, to enact said good. It's as simple as that.

Giving circles, as the natural descendants of *gehs*, *tandas*, and *sou sous*, are charitable practices that have existed for millennia.

The philanthropic sector now acknowledges giving circles as a valid form of philanthropy, and rightly so, as the field is booming. According to *In Abundance: An Analysis of the Thriving Landscape of Collective Giving in the U.S.*, between 2017 and 2023, four thousand giving circles mobilized 370,000 individual donors, who moved $3.1 billion in the United States alone. The number of giving circles tripled between the last landscape survey (which measured the sector between 2007 and 2016) and this one, and the movement is on track to double again in the next five years. These figures are almost certainly a low-ball census, as many circles operate off the books and under the radar. This is a collective giving movement powered by women: 60 percent of the circles in this recent survey are composed of all women, and 84 percent are majority women.[4] The word *sisterhood* comes up a lot when I talk with giving circle folks. Collective giving is a practice deeply rooted in place, meaning giving circle members usually live where they give. They are members of the same communities in which they volunteer, vote, and donate, so they share local knowledge, customs, food, culture, and reference points. And finally, giving circle members are happy. Collective giving improves members' health, wellness, and feelings of agency because collective giving fosters belonging, purpose, and connection to community.

GIVING CIRCLES ARE as varied as the humans who create them. There's Seiji in Brooklyn and his Radfund neighbors who fund community organizing nearby; Lily and her high school peers who raise money for local charities in Tucson, Arizona; Marsha in Birmingham, Alabama, who is a leader in the movement to build giving circles by and for Black communities; and thousands more across the globe. Giving circles raise anywhere from a few hundred dollars annually to millions. Most giving circles in the landscape give more than just their money, expanding the notion of what counts as giving by encompassing the Five T's: time, talent, treasure, testimony, and ties. Some bring together five work colleagues, while others organize hundreds. They can be laser-focused on one issue or locality or identify emerging issues that may change every year. The thing they all have in common, though, is they are groups of people who are practicing philanthropy and civic engagement together.

For the work I do with individuals and foundations, I often use the framework "Me to We to Big We." The idea is that each of us, in order to enter into social change work with integrity, needs to articulate our personal "why." What are our most deeply held values? On whose shoulders do I stand to do this work? What did I learn from my family in terms of generosity, scarcity, and money? What are my powers and how can I use them for good? From this Me position, we can then move to the We. These are the groups and networks we are all part of, like book groups, neighborhood associations, workplace friends, faith-based networks, alumni, professional, fraternal or sororal associations, and giving circles. What is my role in my home, block, school, workplace, even my city? The Big We in America is our democracy. What is my role as a citizen? What might be fairly asked of me in the social contract of my neighborhood, town, state, and country, and what might I ask for in return? Giving circles are an ideal vehicle to have these conversations. Philanthropy is a form of civic engagement, and giving circles provide a way for all of us to engage in this most important work of being citizens.

. . .

YOU MAY HAVE heard the expression "We are our ancestors' wildest dreams." What I love about this idea is the way it pairs both connection to traditional practices and family legacies and future-oriented growth—toward new, better, and stronger ways of living in solidarity and in community.

Like seeds that survive floods and drought, we who practice charity and philanthropy in America have, at our core, a kernel of cultural knowledge. Some of this has its roots in religion—but even as Americans have moved away from organized religion at a rapid pace over the last fifty years, there remains some nugget of these communal mutual aid practices. All of us come from familial, cultural, and faith-based heritages of helping, giving, and making the world a better, fairer, more beautiful place. We learned these traditions from our parents, grandparents, aunties, uncles—our families and communities. We may feel as though we've lost these traditions in the hustle of getting by and getting ahead, but when we take time to reflect, I believe many of us will see how we grew up with them, how we were steeped in them, and how we can pass them on.

Imagine the power that could be unleashed if we reconnected to our cultural heritages of generosity, mutual aid, and helping our neighbors in order to contribute to the civic square. Imagine the power of people getting together in living rooms across the country, putting their minds and hearts together to address local issues, all while breaking bread, sharing a meal, and building community.

Together, we are truly greater than the sum of our parts.

Welcome to the world of giving circles. Come on in.

Part I

ME

The Big Me

They announced it on *Oprah* and the optics were perfect. A young Black mayor with a promising future in the Democratic Party and a not-quite-so-young Republican governor—also with national ambitions—came together on the stage with a twenty-six-year-old tech billionaire. Oprah Winfrey gasped and applauded, as did her audience.

It was 2010, and for years the public education system in Newark, New Jersey, had been plagued by poverty, violence, and underinvestment. That year, less than 40 percent of the city's third- to eighth-grade students were reading or doing math at grade level, and nearly half the district's students were dropping out before finishing high school. The schools were in such bad shape that the state had taken over.[1]

Cory Booker, then mayor of Newark, now a U.S. senator, had secured the cooperation of Governor Chris Christie, as well as a $100 million donation from Facebook founder Mark Zuckerberg. The three were embarking on one of the most audacious exercises in education reform, as described by journalist Dale Russakoff in her book, *The Prize: Who's in Charge of America's Schools?* Russakoff writes, "Their stated goal was not to repair education in Newark but to develop a model for saving it in all of urban America." In five years.[2]

The deal was born in Sun Valley, Idaho, at a swanky dinner hosted by a large financial institution. Booker had arranged to sit next to Zuckerberg, who was rumored to be interested in making big moves in education. Booker's pitch was that Newark was small enough that a $100 million investment would make a difference yet also big enough that it could feasibly serve as a pilot for education reform in other cities.[3] Zuckerberg agreed, on the condition that Booker raise an additional $100 million to match his donation. This would mean $200 million in new funds for Newark's schools. It would also be an audacious first outing for Zuckerberg, a brand-new philanthropist, and a gilded political feather in the cap for Booker.

The 2010s were an era of great reformist zeal in education. *Waiting for "Superman,"* a controversial film about charter schools, came out in 2010. (Bill Gates threw in $2 million for its marketing campaign.)[4] Michelle Rhee, chancellor of District of Columbia Public Schools, was a star in the film and is an exemplar of the reformers of that time. Like many reformists, Rhee was a graduate of Teach for America, begun by Wendy Kopp in the 1990s to send college grads into (usually less well-resourced) public schools across the country with a lot of idealism but only a summer's worth of training. Like other reformsters of that era, Rhee championed school choice, school vouchers, charter schools, tying teachers' salaries to student achievement in test scores, and gutting teacher job protection by ending tenure based on seniority. To many career education folks, Rhee was a smart, unqualified outsider (she'd never run a school, much less a large school district). George Parker, president of the Washington Teachers' Union, said that no superintendent had wrecked morale more than Rhee and that much of her message amounted to teacher-bashing.[5]

School choice, vouchers, and school "portability" (the idea that parents should be able to withdraw from the public school system and use their share of public funding for private or religious school, homeschool, or internet school) are key tenets of education reformists. They're part of a political movement called neoliberalism, which started in the 1970s and sought to turn public goods and monies toward business models, markets, and privatization.

NEOLIBERAL REFORMIST EDUCATION prioritizes choice and incentives over equity and funding, and most often, it is hardest on the poor. Market choices in this arena tend to favor those who have the time, wealth, networks, and wherewithal to plan, coordinate, and move their kids to the best schools for them. The people who benefit the most from privatization are often the rich, as Jason Blakely wrote in *The Atlantic*: "As money is pulled from failing schools and funneled into succeeding ones, wealth can actually be redistributed by the state up the socioeconomic ladder."[6] And that is what happened in Detroit.

Betsy DeVos, appointed secretary of education by President Trump in 2017, is from Detroit and is a fervent advocate for neoliberalizing education. She believes that public education is a monopolistic "dead end" and that the public school system needs to be re-engineered by the government to mimic a market.[7] Starting in the 1990s, DeVos played a big role in getting school choice introduced in Detroit. Over twenty years of marketization has led to a ton of money leaving the public school systems, the closing of many public schools, the funneling of taxpayer dollars toward for-profit charter ventures, poor parents with worse options than richer ones, and no significant improvement in student performance. There are areas of Detroit that are "educational deserts" where families have to travel miles and hours for their kids to attend school.[8]

So, this is the neoliberal context into which Mark Zuckerberg dropped. Add to this amped-up, reformist, ideological zeal the fact that education in the United States was a $667 billion business in 2009 (if you add up all the money that was spent for primary and secondary education in the country during the 2008–2009 school year).[9] And then add to that the national aspirations of two very ambitious politicians and the philanthropic debut of a new billionaire—you can see the fireworks.

LOOKING BACK, it is now clear that the three "heroes" of this story had different objectives. Their shared stated goal was to turn around Newark schools and make this a national model for other urban school districts around the country. But the three had very different ideas regarding *how* to get there. Governor Christie wanted to break the enormous power of the teachers' union. Mayor Booker wanted more charter schools, in keeping with the popular neoliberal dogma of the day. And Zuckerberg wanted to reward good teachers by linking teacher performance to student performance, regardless of teacher seniority, hoping that this would raise the status of teachers generally.[10] Zuckerberg did not know or understand that teacher seniority was, essentially, untouchable in the state at the time. Seniority was nonnegotiable, and dismantling it was the number one priority of the project's primary funder.[11]

Newark spent around $1 billion to run its schools in 2010, so $200 million represented a 20 percent bump. But as they say, the devil is in the details. How would this money get spent and toward which priorities? Pretty much everyone now agrees that the process was terrible from the very start. Parents and teachers in the district found out about this grand experiment happening to their children by tuning in at 4:00 p.m. to watch *Oprah*. They were not consulted on the design or build. In order for Booker to match Zuckerberg's $100 million, he created the Foundation for Newark's Future to run the pilot, but seats on the board went to the wealthy donors who contributed to the match, costing $5 to $10 million annually—well beyond the ability of local community members or community foundations to pay.

But most importantly, the leading roles in this story—Booker, Christie, and Zuckerberg—completely ignored the people who *should* have been the protagonists: the schoolkids in Newark, their parents, and the teachers who knew this system best. These folks were not included or invited and were barely even informed. Dale Russakoff writes that there were many local organizations, teachers' groups, parent groups, and foundations that had been working to improve Newark's schools for years, and they were frozen out of the decision-making body that would allocate this huge influx of cash.

The board decided to spend the money according to a top-down, business-model-minded methodology that had become very popular with education reformists at the time. Over $20 million went to consultants. Some individual education consultants were paid $1,000 per day while teachers earned an extra $3,000 per *year* in the new contract they negotiated, which worked out to roughly $10 per hour when you factor in all the extra time they had to put in. In an interview with Terry Gross on NPR, Rusakoff says, "Well, that was another case of . . . this enormous gap between the people who have come to save the Newark children and the people who actually cared for and taught the Newark children."[12]

Because the people in charge of the great experiment were not community members, the implementation was tone-deaf. Newark had been a community where most kids walked to their local public schools; there was not a busing system in place except for the kids who were bused to special-needs schools. Instituting school choice meant that, overnight, parents had to go online and pick among sixty schools—some district schools, some charter schools. At the same time, the new superintendent (imported from New York City) was closing, consolidating, and rearranging schools. All this was a huge disruption to the way parents, kids, families, and teachers had experienced school for generations. And it was done without their participation, consent, or input.[13]

Russakoff said, "I think it shows why this really has to be a process that is rooted in the community and has its strong advocates who aren't going anywhere, who are going to stay there and believe in it, year after year, and work for it. It's not something that's going to happen in five years or . . . within the term of a mayor or a governor. It's something that's going to take generations and has to be worked at continually."[14] The Foundation for Newark's Future closed in 2016, and the five-year experiment was over. For the technocrats and billionaires who don't send their kids to public schools in Newark, this experiment cost money, maybe there were some lessons learned, but it's mostly an "oh well." But for the families, students, and educators in Newark, this experiment was highly disruptive and, in some cases, a serious setback for kids. Five years wasted in a child's primary education is an incalculable loss for that child and her family.

In a 2018 interview, Ras Baraka, a school principal, son of poet and activist Amiri Baraka, and an activist who opposed this project and later became the mayor of Newark, called the whole thing problematic because outsiders "parachuted" in instead of meaningfully engaging the community.[15] As a concrete example of think tank solutions not being in touch with reality, the foundation advised the district to lay off attendance counselors to save money at a time when many schools were suffering from chronic absenteeism. The Foundation for Newark's Future, full of outside experts, never took the time to truly understand local issues, so it sent resources to the wrong places.

In the end, according to two academic studies (one paid for by Zuckerberg and the other commissioned by someone who helped administer the pilot), the Newark experiment was, at best, a modest success. After initially dipping, math and reading test scores have gone up a little. The $200 million infusion did win some concessions from the teachers' union as regards to tenure and test-based accountability metrics, partly because $31 million of that went to paying teachers' overdue and much-deserved backpay. Newark's charter schools received $57.6 million, and they used it to double the enrollment of children into the city's charter schools. And in the case of Newark, Russakoff says this is good for children.[16] Charter schools in Newark dramatically outperform the district schools, even though statewide this is not the case (nor is it the case nationally). Charter schools in Newark are able to get more dollars to benefit kids as compared to district schools (which have a more entrenched bureaucracy and union-ized teachers), so they were able to use more of the cash influx to provide social services, counseling, social workers, teachers' aides, and so on directly to students. In the end, Russakoff would love to see this trend reversed: to give increased funding to non-charter public schools within school districts, because they know best what their students need.

Ten years later, the city's charter system is thriving, and the district public schools that serve over half of Newark's schoolchildren face debilitating budget cuts.[17] Those on the "it worked" side cite modest improvements in test scores and increased enrollment in charter schools. Those on the "it didn't work" side cite lack of meaningful community engagement and disinvestment in unionized district schools.

No one thinks the Foundation for Newark's Future experiment was a roaring success. No one is replicating it. It has not become a national model to reimagine the nation's public schools. Its measurable successes were meager. The charter school system in Newark appears to be the big winner, and while some charters are providing good educations for children, they do so by taking public money away from public school districts, without public oversight or accountability.

Booker, Christie, and Zuckerberg made a critical mistake by not consulting the people who knew the most and had the biggest stake: Newark's parents, education professionals, and community leaders. Their biggest mistake was thinking they knew it all. Their biggest mistake was hubris.

Within three years, Cory Booker and Chris Christie had moved on to other bigger things. Booker became a U.S. senator; Christie ran for president of the United States twice. Zuckerberg went back to the West Coast, got married, and with his wife, Priscilla Chan, formed the Chan Zuckerberg Initiative (CZI). Starting in 2017, CZI has made nine-figure investments in technology and education, betting that personalized computerized learning journeys for children would catapult them into the ninety-eighth percentile on standardized tests. After about six years of investing in technology to vastly improve how education is delivered, CZI laid off much of its education program staff in the summer of 2023. It's a tacit admission that their tech-in-education strategy hasn't lived up to their hopes.

WE'VE SEEN A LOT of the myth of American individualism recently, with President Trump declaring during his first term, "I alone can fix this," and Brett Kavanaugh declaring during his Supreme Court nomination process that he'd "done it all on my own." Grit. Perseverance. Bootstraps. These are all part of the ideology of American individualism. In philanthropic spaces, this obsession with individualism leads to a hyperfocus on the donor. When the social good sector focuses on the makers of social change, this myth of individualism tends to anoint heroes rather than contemplating the more complex truth that it is usually a collective effort that brings change. Rosa Parks is duly and rightfully famous for refusing to give up her seat, but the Montgomery bus boycott was months in the organizing, and it gained national attention and began to move the needle when thousands of additional citizens joined the year-long boycott.

The myth of American individualism is exactly that—a myth. Most of us have had a leg up, a helping hand from family members, mentors, a boss, coaches. In Supreme Court Justice Brett Kavanaugh's case, his leg up included being a legacy at Yale (his father and grandfather both went there), his education in an affluent suburb with excellent schools (Bethesda, Maryland), plus growing up with two parents who were both lawyers in a family wealthy enough to afford private school. He didn't do it "all on his own." He might very well have worked hard, but he also had tons of help.

To build the Donors of Color Network, I interviewed 150 wealthy people of color across the United States. These were folks who'd *all* experienced racism, discrimination, and bias because of the color of their skin, accents, country of origin, or religion. And not a single one of them ascribed their considerable success to their own effort alone. One interviewee, a Black man in his late thirties, put it best, saying, "Bootstraps is bullshit."

That man, an investment banker by trade, credits his extended family, friends, and colleagues—plus his own good fortune and hard work—for his success. He and his mother immigrated to the United States from Jamaica, where their family has lived in the same community for over one hundred years. The importance of owning real estate was drilled into this young man from an early age, and he and his mother own properties in an increasingly expensive part of Brooklyn, New York. He told me, "The real source of my wealth is that a lot of people have given a lot to me over time. I hate people who talk about pulling themselves up by their bootstraps—I think that doesn't exist. I am the result of a huge amount of people helping me, pulling me. I've ended up in a field where the compensation is above average. I am not that talented. I'm good at what I do. I'm pretty proficient . . . So yeah, I guess I'm self-made, but with the help of a lot of others."

The myth of American individualism is simplistic and sentimental. It is not only untruthful, it is harmful. It lays blame and places responsibility on individuals for what are truly vast, systemic forces—like poverty, redlining, iniquitous public schools, or a biased criminal justice system. It ignores systems that have brutalized groups of people. It evacuates the past and makes us feel like we alone are responsible and that we alone have to figure it out. Those who are born with privileges get to feel like they alone "did it" while at the same time working hard to preserve for their children the very same systems that benefited them.

Big Phil buys right into the myth of American individualism. The wealthy donor is the sun king in Big Phil's philanthropic galaxy; he's also the smartest guy in the room. In Newark, Big Phil partnered up with two ambitious big politicians to assert their top-down, expert-knows-best billionaire will with negative results for the public school parents and children who were the targets of their largesse.

THE BILL & MELINDA GATES FOUNDATION is the largest private foundation in the world with an endowment valued at $75.2 billion as of December 31, 2023. It also spent billions to improve education in the United States. In the early 2000s, a few years before Zuckerberg's crusade in New Jersey, it poured $650 million into breaking up big "failing" schools into smaller schools, on the unproven theory that small ones serve children better than big ones. In 2009, Bill Gates acknowledged that this hadn't worked the way he'd wanted it to. But in some cases, the foundation's experiment had actually harmed students. Denver's Manual High School shut down after Gates funding was pulled and students were shipped to other schools around the city. Their graduation rates dropped. Only half of them went on to graduate, and they'd been forced to leave a school that had previously had a graduation rate of 68 percent.[18] William Schambra of the Bradley Center for Philanthropy and Civic Renewal had just visited Milwaukee, another project site, and he commented, "For Gates it's fine to say, well, that was an interesting experiment and it didn't work out, and walk away from it. But for Milwaukee . . . those are real children we're talking about. For the folks in Seattle, it's an 'oopsie,' but for folks in Milwaukee, it's a major disruption."[19]

The foundation then moved to funding the development of the Common Core State Standards initiative with the Obama administration. Around the same time, it spent $355 million pushing a teacher-evaluation system based on standardized testing that the creator of the system said wasn't meant to be used that way.[20] Bill Gates wrote in later reports that neither program had worked. One education initiative that the foundation said *had* worked is the Gates Millennium Scholars Program, which provided full college scholarships to twenty thousand students of color. After sixteen years, they've discontinued the program because they seek larger-scale results.[21] The *Los Angeles Times* went on to write an editorial excoriating philanthropists who are not education experts (even if they hire education experts), and the public officials who listen to them, for setting a public agenda for the nation's public schools.[22]

To be fair, the Bill & Melinda Gates Foundation has had heroic and remarkable success vaccinating children in poor countries. It invested $1.5 billion to buy vaccines, which created an incentive for Big Pharma to get in on the action. The number of manufacturers involved in vaccine research jumped from three to twelve.[23] Gavi, the Vaccine Alliance, heavily supported by Gates, guaranteed it would buy millions of doses. Within five years, 99 million people were vaccinated, averting an estimated 1.7 million deaths. Thanks to the Bill & Melinda Gates Foundation, it is estimated that 8 million children have been saved from unnecessary deaths in the years up to 2020.[24] That is truly amazing work.

The Gates Foundation spends more annually on global health than does the government of Germany. Its scale is so large it sits alongside countries in these conversations. The foundation spent

$2 billion on malaria, and since it began investing in this area, malaria deaths are down 42 percent since 2000. The foundation then turned its attention to polio. In 1988, a thousand children a day were paralyzed by polio. Thirty years later, after Gates gave $3 billion toward an $11 billion initiative by the World Health Organization (WHO), 2.5 billion children have been vaccinated and cases of polio have been cut by 99.9 percent. Polio has been virtually eradicated among the 1.3 billion people of India, the most populous country on the planet.[25]

The Gates Foundation is now the second-largest donor to the WHO, second only to the U.S. government. Millions of lives have been saved, and that is indisputably good. There are critiques, however, that have to do with one very rich human exerting such outsize influence on global health. Bill Gates's personal intuition and his proclivity to solve complex issues with technology can lead him to target more "easy-fix" solutions. He tends to dismiss underlying systems that get to root causes of poverty and disease in poorer countries. His huge influence can unbalance global spending on health and other areas, like agriculture. His wealth is sometimes derived from industries that harm communities in which the foundation does its social good. For example, regarding the picking and choosing of more "easy-fix" solutions, chronic diseases hardly appear in the foundation's portfolio. The medical journal *The Lancet* writes of an "alarmingly poor correlation between the Foundation's funding and childhood disease priorities."[26] Gates is keen on technical solutions but less interested in strengthening the healthcare infrastructure needed to deliver vaccinations on the ground. That changed somewhat after the Ebola crisis of 2014, but in general, the foundation doesn't like to invest in systems, which may offer better long-term solutions, preferring instead to find and fund technical endpoint solves.

Finally, like many wealthy people, Gates's financial investments can be at counter purposes to their charity. For example, Gates funded polio and measles vaccinations in Nigeria while holding investments in oil companies that were polluting the Niger Delta. Digging for oil created oil bore holes full of stagnant water that created ideal breeding grounds for the mosquitoes that spread malaria. Also the resulting toxic oil flares poisoned the air, which caused higher rates of asthma nearby and blurred children's vision. And the floods of oil workers and the soldiers who were needed to protect them from rebel guerrillas attracted prostitution, which led to a surge in HIV and teenage pregnancy, both of which were also targets of Gates's charitable campaigns.[27] The Gates Foundation has since changed its investing criteria, but it remains one of the world's largest investors in biotechnology for farming and pharmaceuticals. Perhaps the biggest critique is the long-term sustainability one. What happens if the Gates Foundation pulls its funding or shifts its focus? Looking at malaria, while foreign aid has cut worldwide malaria deaths by three quarters, more than eight hundred African children die every day from the disease, and malaria deaths globally have remained steady since 2016. India and Mozambique came close to eliminating malaria but have seen rates rise again after foreign aid was withdrawn.[28] Hopefully the Gates Foundation stays the course on global health, unlike with its experiments in education.

But ultimately, is it wise for the rest of us to depend on one very wealthy person to have such a big influence on the global health agenda, what gets researched and funded, where, and how? I don't think so.

. . .

THOMAS SIEBEL is well known for founding Siebel Systems, sell-
ing it to his former employer Oracle (making Siebel a billionaire),
surviving an elephant attack that almost cost him a leg, and starting the Montana Meth Project. Siebel spends part of every year at
his ranch in Montana, which, like many rural states, has suffered
greatly from a methamphetamine problem. Meth is highly addic-
tive and highly destructive (see *Breaking Bad*). In 2005, Montana
had the fifth-worst meth problem among all the U.S. states. The
drug was costing the state $300 million per year, with the costs
to families and individuals immeasurably greater.[29] According to
state officials, meth was responsible for 80 percent of the prison
population—90 percent for female inmates—and about half the
state's foster care population.[30]

Siebel created the Meth Project in 2005 (now known as the
Montana Meth Project) to "unsell" meth to kids. He sought
out creative ad agencies and Hollywood directors to create
ads that were so gross, upsetting, and gut-wrenching that kids
would never use meth, "Not Even Once," as one ad campaign
memorably emphasized. This type of intervention is known
as a demand-side intervention because it is aimed at potential
users, rather than suppliers. The campaign was designed to reach
80 percent of Montana teens with at least three ads per week. The
ads are terrifying—in one, a young girl picks scabs on her face, in
another a boy kicks his mom as he steals money from her purse,
in another a young teen prostitutes herself, another features blood
and rotting teeth. Siebel's annual investment of $2 million (cheap,
relatively speaking!) made the project the biggest ad buyer in the
state (TV, radio, billboards). Seven other states have adopted a
similar strategy, and it was named the third-most effective philanthropy in the world (whatever that means) by *Barron's* magazine

in 2010. The Montana legislature threw in $1 million of public money to support what had been a privately funded campaign.[31] Siebel's campaign served as a catalyst for further funding and similar projects. So it was a success, right?

One would think that before a campaign can act as a catalyst, it ought to be proven to be effective. So where's the data that says the Montana Meth Project has worked? There are three academic journal studies that I could find, and all three say, in a word, *meh*. A 2008 article in *Prevention Science* is pretty damning: "There is no evidence that reductions in methamphetamine use in Montana are caused by the advertising campaign. On the basis of current evidence, continued public funding and rollout of Montana-style methamphetamine programs is inadvisable."[32] A University of Montana professor used data from the CDC's (Centers for Disease Control and Prevention) biennial Youth Risk Behavior Surveillance System and found little evidence that the Montana Meth Project curbed meth use among high school students.[33] A 2014 follow-up study also by the University of Montana adds limply that the project may have reduced meth use among some white high school students.[34]

Despite scant evidence and very mixed reviews, the *Stanford Social Innovation Review* still dubbed Siebel a hero.[35]

ZUCKERBERG, GATES, AND SIEBEL were just doing what guys like them have always done—go west, young man! Found a religion! A cult! A homestead! A city on the hill! U.S. history is full of stories, fictional and not, of men striking out with grandiose ambitions that lionize individuality. And this cultural predilection sets up the way billionaires like Zuckerberg, Gates, and Siebel solve problems today.

I do not want to disparage the amazing spark of a great idea, or the role that individuals can play in inventing, innovating, creating, and building. But in the social-change sphere, which is fueled, in part, by philanthropy, the hero's "I alone can fix it" mentality is simply not enough. Billionaire, entrepreneurial, individual philanthropists are no match for the scale of the immense problems we face. It's just not smart to rely on any individual, no matter how wealthy or well-intentioned, to fix systemic and complex problems. Especially if those underlying systems helped that person get so rich in the first place. Even worse, relying on these wealthy individuals can inspire a sort of passivity among the rest of us. And our system doesn't work when we are passive.

As mentioned earlier, in the world of global public health, Bill Gates is so rich and he gives so much money that his influence is on par with governments. He sits at the table with the same gravitational force (if it were measured in U.S. dollars) as entire tax bases of entire countries. In some ways, the fact that he, as an example of Big Phil, gets to play that role points to a failure of governments to vaccinate their populations. Big Phil stepping in helps children get vaccinated, say, but Big Phil is only human, so his intervention might be more whimsical or short-lived than a government's. And Big Phil ought never be an excuse for a government to be derelict in its duty to its citizens. Big Phil steps in when states don't, and that is not a good thing for those of us who live in states.

I'VE WORKED WITH the Gates Foundation on several projects, including to build the donors of color research and network, and philanthropy curricula that centers values, equity, and fairness. The staffers with whom I've collaborated are, almost to a person, whip smart, kind, thoughtful, quirky, lovely people. They are truly cherished colleagues, and some of them, friends. They (and my team and I) are aware of the contradictions and tensions of working within a behemoth of a foundation while also trying to nudge it to evolve, of working within a system rife with inequities while also trying to drive many more resources toward human flourishing. I think they, and we, see the incredible opportunity because of the foundation's positionality and massive size. I critique the Gates Foundation as a friend and comrade traveler, an auntie even, who believes it can do even better.

WHILE I'VE PICKED on Bill Gates, Mark Zuckerberg, and Thomas Siebel here, at least these guys are trying to do good. They're tackling big issues like public education, meth addiction, and eradicable diseases in the hopes of making lives better for millions of non-billionaire people. I may disagree with their top-down, technocratic methods and points of view and the disproportionate influence they wield because of their heft, but on many points, I'm on their side, at least part of the time.

There is a whole posse of other billionaires who are throwing their resources and influence at serving themselves and their wealthy peers. They are intent on preserving financial systems that help them build even more wealth while their philanthropy focuses on helping their businesses, dismantling public education, taking away voting rights, and restricting access to healthcare. Their goal is to shrink the public sphere, take away opportunities for working families, take away access to voting rights and bodily autonomy rights. They want to shrink the state (the government) so that they, the richest among us, can exert even more control and take even more of our common resources. If I care about expanding, these folks are intent on contracting. So while I've taken some swipes at a few, for this crew, I'd need battalions.

For the purposes of this book, in the social-change sphere, the only thing that a wealthy person can do that *only* a wealthy person can do is to organize, influence, and nudge their wealthy peers. Wealthy people listen to other wealthy people, more than they'll listen to curated lists, content experts, or even their own hired, paid staff and advisors. Influencing and organizing one's peers is a critically important role because doing this can bring many more resources, hearts, minds, and networks to bear. Doing so is also a tacit admission that "I alone" cannot fix it, and that in order to bring about social change, we need each other.

THE MYTHICAL, LONE HERO story tends to crumble when applied in real life to the complex, communal work of making social change.

Ironically, for all the attention we pay them, most billionaires aren't all that generous. *Forbes* looked at the four hundred wealthiest Americans and gave them a score, from 1 (least generous) to 5 (most generous). They looked at "money out the door," so didn't count money that people have parked in their own private foundations or tax-advantaged donor-advised funds (DAFs).[36] Most members of the *Forbes* 400 scored a 1 or a 2, meaning they have donated less than 5 percent of their fortune to charity so far. Only nine of the four hundred scored a 5, meaning they've given away more than 20 percent of their fortunes. These nine are Bill Gates, Melinda French Gates, MacKenzie Scott, Warren Buffett, George Soros, Gordon Moore, Amos Hostetter Jr., Lynn Schusterman, and John Arnold.[37]

Also, billionaire pet causes can shift with the wind. Case in point is the NoVo Foundation, founded by Jennifer and Peter

Buffett in 1997. Peter is the youngest son of legendary billionaire investor Warren Buffett, who pledged Berkshire Hathaway stock valued at $1.4 billion to the budding philanthropists. NoVo quickly made a name for itself, investing significant multiyear grants in feminist, social justice, people of color–led organizations and movements in the United States and abroad. NoVo became foundational backbone supporters of an entire ecosystem of organizations and movements that were fighting for gender equality, and it won awards for doing philanthropy in a more trusting, community-minded, less top-down way.

Looking at Peter and Jennifer Buffett's public statements, they seem to have been earnest and sincere about moving feminist and equity-minded values in their giving. They were smart to focus on women and girls because women and girls receive a tiny percentage of philanthropy's largesse, 1.9 percent.[38] For women and girls of color, it's even worse. In 2017, grantmaking to organizations serving women and girls of color amounted to 0.5 percent of philanthropy in the United States.[39] So NoVo adding their heft and influence to that small ecosystem of underfunded but important work felt monumental.

But it didn't last. In May 2020, at the height of the COVID pandemic, the NoVo Foundation announced it would drop two major grantmaking programs, end multiyear funding, review its entire portfolio of grants, and lay off almost half its staff. As of that date, NoVo had made grants of over $700 million toward causes like ending the sexual trafficking of girls, boosting adolescent girls' health and wellness, and ending violence against women and girls. According to a researcher at the National Center for Responsive Philanthropy (NCRP), from the years 2016 to 2018, NoVo was responsible for 17 percent of all domestic funding for women's rights and human services specifically for women, and 37 percent of funding in those categories for Black women.[40] Grantee partners were stunned and scared, especially as they grappled with the life-and-death issues faced by their clients during the pandemic. Reaction was swift and devastating; people decried this sudden and swift disinvestment from the lives and safety of women and girls during COVID. Communications from NoVo were lackluster and unspecific. The Buffetts blamed a market downturn (which would affect the value of their expected Berkshire Hathaway stock transfer) but, more importantly, acknowledged a "philosophical shift" that underlay their decision. As quoted in the *Chronicle of Philanthropy*, Buffett said, "We're a dynamic organization. I'm out there listening all the time, trying to learn and grow."[41]

In 2020, *Inside Philanthropy* awarded "Trainwreck of the Year" to the NoVo Foundation's "Change of Heart," writing that this blowup should serve as a "devastating reminder that even the most generous benefactors can always pull the rug from underneath you."[42]

It now seems obvious that this earthquake could have been foretold by watching where the couple moved. In 2010, Peter and Jennifer Buffett had relocated from New York City to a nineteenth-century farmhouse on fifty acres of prime farmland in Kingston, New York, about ninety minutes north of the city in the Hudson Valley. At the time of the funding disruption, Peter said that the couple had decided to shift their grantmaking to be in support of "building vibrant, equitable, and joyful communities,"[43] and almost $200 million of that (the number is likely higher, but NoVo does not release an annual report, and much of its giving is anonymized via donor-advised funds) has gone to the community that they now happen to live in: Kingston, New York.

Sidebar note on donor advised funds, which are commonly called DAFs. DAFs are like charitable checking accounts. The person making the donation gets the full tax benefit for making a charitable donation immediately upon putting money into their DAF, but there is no requirement that the money go out the door charitably beyond the minimum 5 percent per year. While most DAF accounts in the United States hold under $100,000 in assets, all together, DAF assets reached nearly $229 billion in 2022, while grants made from DAFs amounted to $52 billion.[44] Fidelity Charitable is the world's largest DAF sponsor (meaning they're a financial institution that can hold and administer DAFs), which makes them, essentially, the world's largest grantmaker.

Going back to Kingston, New York, the NoVo Foundation has bought a 1,255-acre farm, an AM/FM radio station, and a building that now houses a nonprofit food cooperative.[45] NoVo prints local currency (by all accounts gorgeous) and is the predominant or exclusive funder of Kingston's local news media and radio station, a museum, a think tank, a mutual aid network, a healthcare network, a hospital, the Kingston City Land Bank, the YMCA, the community center, and dozens of nonprofits.[46] One NoVo grant recipient who also is a local said, "They've invested more money than the actual budget of the City of Kingston, without there being any sort of democratic process."[47]

Kingston boomed when IBM chose the city as its headquarters in the 1950s, then it went bust in 1995 when IBM announced it was leaving. As a one-company town, Kingston residents saw a 20 percent drop in income after IBM left Ulster County.[48] What will happen to Kingston if/when the Buffetts decide to move? Of course, it's their money and they can do what they wish with it, but because of their outsize wealth, the Buffetts exerted outsize influence in the gender-equity funding space and, now, in the quickly gentrifying town of Kingston, New York.

What they're doing in Kingston sounds utopian (maybe especially for them), and in a funny way, maybe the Buffett couple want to be more proximate to the community they now serve and live in. But they do bear some responsibility as backbone, foundational supporters of the organizations they used to support. It's been difficult for the women's and girls' organizations they used to fund to find new funders, and NoVo did a poor job preparing (or even communicating with) them for the transition. They might, in fact, bear an extra dose of responsibility and accountability because of their outsize wealth and influence.

The Novo Foundation exemplifies a sad truth: Big Phil is undemocratic because it is publicly accountable to no one.

As for Kingston, wouldn't it be better if the Buffetts just paid more taxes—they've moved most of their civic largesse via 501(c)(3) vehicles, which are tax-exempt—so that their giving could go through some sort of democratic process?

Of NoVo's millions being poured into Kingston, Peter Buffett wrote in a social media post, "I am coming to terms with how much power I have. This is new to me, especially when so many have become dependent on NoVo's resources. We have a responsibility, and we will try to meet it. And probably be imperfect about it."[49] Peter was born in 1958, and though he was a musician and lived a sort of scrappy early adulthood, he inherited $10 million in 2004 when his mother died. When Peter was forty-eight, his father gave him and Jennifer the initial gift of $1 billion in stock, making them co-presidents of one of the world's biggest philanthropies. He muses on social media and shares sometimes surprisingly vulnerability. Even with earnest humility, a billionaire's constant learning comes with costs and consequences when it is done live, involving complex social issues and in community with other humans.

FINALLY, DON'T COUNT on billionaires to actually change anything. As Anand Giridharadas wrote in his 2018 book *Winners Take All: The Elite Charade of Changing the World*, extremely wealthy people are not incentivized to change the very systems that made them very, very wealthy to begin with. They are incentivized to maintain those systems that enriched them.

Philanthropy can walk hand in hand with Big Phil, creating clever vehicles to transform Big Phil into Big Me. Philanthropy can help burnish Big Phil's halo (and his ego) and pave over some of his misdeeds. Private family foundations and other vehicles created to support philanthropy benefit from the U.S. tax code in ways that make Big Phil even bigger. Keep in mind that foundations in the United States hold $1.5 trillion in assets, and DAFs hold an additional $229 billion.[50] Big Phil can even make a donation to his own private foundation or DAF and get the full tax deduction for doing so. And without values-driven action and intention, these vehicles can become great hordes of wealth that accumulate tax-free.

We the public pay when dollars get deposited into private foundations and DAFs and stay there. Those dollars are not in circulation buying goods and services or being invested, many of those dollars are not out there doing the charitable good they were set aside to do, and the taxes that would've been paid on that money never gets used to build roads, fund public schools, pay for the police department, and the like. Because of this usurpation of public good for private gain, one of my friends who is a law professor calls private family foundations and DAFs "taking organizations" rather than "giving organizations." By taking advantage of banking, tax, and regulatory systems in perfectly legal ways, Big Phil can bloat into Big Me.

There are some inspiring and notable exceptions, like Yvon Chouinard, the eighty-three-year-old founder of Patagonia who gave away the company and is a billionaire no longer.[51] He transformed Patagonia into what is essentially a foundation for environmental purposes, saying, "The earth is our only shareholder as of now."[52] In 2024, two billionaires, Ruth Gottesman and Michael Bloomberg, made billion-dollar donations to two medical schools, Albert Einstein College of Medicine in the Bronx and Johns Hopkins University in Baltimore, respectively, to make medical school tuition free for most. Jen and David Risher founded #HalfMyDAF to peer-pressure other wealthy people to give away a lot more than the 5 percent minimum. A group of wealthy individuals known as the Patriotic Millionaires came together in 2010 to protest the Bush-era tax cuts for rich people. They want three things: higher tax on millionaires, equal political representation for all Americans, and a living wage for working people. As Morris Pearl, former managing director at BlackRock and Patriotic Millionaires chair, says on the group's website, "I'm not any more altruistic than the next guy, I'm just greedy for a different kind of country than most other rich people. I want to be a rich man in a rich country."[53] Erica Payne, president and founder of Patriotic Millionaires, closes her introductory letter in their book, *Tax the Rich! How Lies, Loopholes, and Lobbyists Make the Rich Even Richer*, with, "Tax the rich; save America. Let's get started."[54]

We know how to change the tax system so that it is fairer, and this is a broadly popular desire on the part of most Americans.

What we lack is the political will to do so. And many of the people who like the system the way it is, and who pay to keep it that
way, well, they're millionaires.

Collecting taxes to level the playing field and to pay for
society-wide benefits is an ancient, even biblical, idea. In his
address to a delegation from Italy's revenue agency in January
2022, Pope Francis said, "In reality, taxation is a sign of legal-
ity and justice." He half-jokingly noted that while tax collectors
may never win a popularity contest, their work is vital for the
functioning of a fair society. He urged everyone to pay their fair
share of taxes, particularly the wealthy, so that the poor would
not be crushed by the more economically hefty. He closed by
reminding the tax collectors of Italy that they have a patron saint,
Saint Matthew the Apostle, who was a publican, or tax collector
in Roman times, before he decided to follow Jesus.[55]

Even though this book is about collective giving, philanthropy,
and civic engagement, these activities are deeply intertwined with
other monetary systems, like taxation and private capital. Let's
put the dollars moved in these different arenas into some context.
In 2022, Americans gave $499 billion to charitable organizations
in the United States.[56] The same year, the U.S. federal government budget was $6.272 trillion;[57] and U.S. capital markets were
worth approximately $50.8 trillion.[58] In other words, the U.S.
government allocated more than twenty times more dollars than
philanthropy did, and U.S. capital markets moved one hundred
times more dollars. If philanthropy is human-size, U.S. government expenditures are hippo-size and U.S. capital markets are
Tyrannosaurus rex–sized.[59] The financial power of philanthropy is
dwarfed by both capital markets and government expenditures.

We have a very complex tax system that funds the U.S. government, and most Americans think the current tax code that

favors the very wealthy over the rest of us is unfair. A majority of Americans are bothered by the feeling that wealthy people and corporations do not pay their fair share of taxes and think taxes on these groups should be raised.[60] Thanks to a tax code that vastly favors investment income over earned income (like wages or salary from a job), billionaires pay a lower tax rate than most teachers and retail workers. The very wealthy are also able to pay for accountants and lawyers who help them cleverly avoid taxes, so in the end, they end up paying a smaller percentage of their income in taxes than most working families. On top of that, according to American Compass, a conservative policy think tank, the very wealthy add to their wealth at three times the rate of the rest of us.[61]

All this contributes to the growing wealth gap in the United States. According to the nonpartisan Congressional Budget Office, income inequality in the United States has been rising for decades, with the incomes of the highest group of earners rapidly outpacing the rest of the population.[62] Moreover, inequality in the United States is rising faster than in other rich nations. There's something called the Gini coefficient, which measures a country's economic inequality. It ranges from zero (completely equal) to one hundred (completely unequal). The United States' Gini coefficient has been steadily going up. It was 39.8 in 2023, right around where Jamaica and Bulgaria score,[63] and significantly higher than that of Canada, France, and Germany—according to the Organization for Economic Cooperation and Development (OECD), a consortium of advanced economies.

Oxfam, Patriotic Millionaires, the Institute for Policy Studies, and the Fight Inequality Alliance, organizations that are concerned about growing wealth inequality, released a report in early 2023 that found that creating a federal U.S. wealth tax could raise more than $583 billion annually. The individuals who would have to pay more would include the 64,500 people in the United States with more than $50 million in wealth, and the 728 billionaires who reside here.[64] For scale, President Biden's 2022 student debt–relief program would cost $30 billion annually.[65] And primary and secondary education for the entire country is pretty close to the potential gain, about $600 billion per year.

Seems like a no-brainer to me. If our government paid for great public schools, philanthropy wouldn't have to. And on a personal level, imagine the emotional and mental space that would get freed up if you didn't have to worry so much about health insurance or paying for a medical emergency, elder care, or childcare. How many of us have had to stay in jobs we didn't like because of health insurance or declined a more entrepreneurial path because of the cost of health insurance. I know I have. Half of my nonprofit salary went to childcare at one point when my kids were too young for kindergarten. I needed that job for its health insurance. Many of my friends are helping to take care of aging parents. Every family has to figure it out on their own; I know I'd love to have access to a larger system of support, help, and care for my brother and me to help our parents age healthily and well.

We live in the richest country in the world. I'd happily pay higher taxes so that my fellow citizens and I could share some of the dividends in the form of a strong social safety net that was the envy of the rest of the world. And I sincerely doubt that doing so would dampen the entrepreneurial spirit of this place either.

One of my giving circle sisters, Chitra Aiyar, is an activist, organizer, and tax attorney. Chitra astutely observed that taxes are like a giant giving circle—you put money in, you don't get to decide where it all goes, but you get to voice your opinion, advocate, and vote. I don't like all the ways my tax dollars are spent, but I can vote for initiatives and candidates that reflect my vision of the society I want to live in. It's on all of us to exercise our civic engagement muscles, voice, and vote to advocate for the ways we want our tax dollars to be allocated. With the Asian Women Giving Circle, we put our money in and argue, discuss, and vote for which projects and organizations will get that year's funding. The funding does not always go to the project or organization I vote for and sometimes I'm very sad about it. Of course, as an individual, I can send money to the places that don't get funded. But each individual circle member, or citizen in the case of paying taxes, has to take the lumps along with the wins.

Both are by design a sublimation of the individual (me and you) for the common good (we and us).

THE MYTH OF American individuals is enduring. We love to find and lift up exceptional stories of exceptional people doing exceptional things. I'm as susceptible to these inspiring stories as anyone—and certainly, there are many extraordinary individuals doing things that deserve recognition. But the problem is, these individuals are the exception, and their successes are often a distraction from the hard work of collaboration that's typically required to make real change.

In my field of philanthropy, we *love* to anoint heroes. We can't dismiss the efforts of those wealthy donors who are making good-faith attempts to practice philanthropy differently—and there are some good ones!—but ultimately, when it comes to durable social change, focusing on individual heroes is inadequate.

We are in an all-hands-on-all-decks moment that requires not just an individual, but a collective and systemic response. There are many big, hairy problems we, as humanity, face. Look at the Sustainable Development Goals (SDGs) developed by the UN General Assembly in 2015. There are seventeen of them, including ending poverty, ending hunger, and ensuring quality education for all.[66] And this list doesn't even get to things like the criminal justice system in the United States, rising authoritarianism here and globally, the importance of separating church and state, the importance of a free and fair press, wars against oppressed people, global pandemics, and more.

For all their billions in assets and billions spent, philanthropy hasn't made a dent on these critical goals. Part of the reason why is that it's been mostly technocratic, top-down, billionaire-led Big Phil that has been leading the philanthropic charge. To make any headway on any of these big hairies, it's going to take all of us—governments, elected officials, nongovernmental organizations, nonprofits, research arms, legal entities, advocacy groups, and regular citizens who are educated and care enough to take actions to be part of the solutions.

Regular people—you and me—are important at every step along any social change arc. Take, for example, vaccinations. Of course, scientists, public health officials, and vaccine manufacturers are critical. But regular people will identify the barriers to getting the vaccinations and can figure out how best to get vaccinations into arms. Community members can alert public health officials about any false information that might be circulating and can help deliver culturally competent and locally legible ways to fight fear with facts. Community leaders might volunteer to get vaccinated first to allay those fears and build buy-in. They might devise a public narrative campaign of some sort to spread the word and normalize medical intervention.

Systemic problems require systemic solutions, which means government officials, private sector leaders, researchers, journalists and writers, artists, activists, advocates, teachers, and regular people are all rowing together at least some of the time.

Individual billionaire philanthropists are not enough. Philanthropy alone is not enough because no matter how much we raise, it will never come close to the money moved by tax codes or stock markets. The problem with focusing on an individual donor's intent is that it's only half the story, and arguably, it's the wrong half. It's time to change the subject away from the donor and move from the Me to the We, our communities, and to the Big We, our very democracy.

2

When You Think of a Philanthropist, Who Do You See?

Remember that the word *philanthropy* comes from two Greek words: *philos* meaning "love" and *anthropos* meaning "man or humanity," so together, the word *philanthropy* is the "love of humanity."

Today, the word *philanthropy* usually conjures wealthy people going to charitable galas or endowing museums, hospitals, and other monuments to private wealth transformed into public goods. Since ancient times, wealthy patrons and priests have used their money to build temples and houses of worship; philanthropy and faith have been intertwined since the time of the pharaohs. Modern philanthropy, as a professional field and sector in the United States, was born out of the great wealth accumulation and accompanying wealth disparity during the late nineteenth and early twentieth centuries.[1] America's first gilded age saw the rise of industrial titans whose names still adorn the legacy foundations, public libraries, concert halls, hospitals, and universities they started. To name just a few, the Carnegie Corporation is a philanthropic foundation begun by steel and rail magnate Andrew Carnegie in 1911, the Rockefeller Foundation was founded by oil tycoon John D. Rockefeller in 1913, and the Ford Foundation was founded in 1936 by Henry Ford and his son, Edsel. Fun fact: Milburn Pennybags, the tuxedoed guy scampering off with a bag of money in the game Monopoly is modeled after J. P. Morgan, the banker and philanthropist.

Big Phil is a great-great-grandchild of that storied period in U.S. history. Big Phil's milieu is our own modern gilded age, similarly bedeviled by an extreme contrast between the very wealthy and the very poor and similarly populated by impossibly wealthy individuals who have started eponymous philanthropic endeavors like the Gates Foundation (formerly known as the Bill & Melinda Gates Foundation) and the Chan Zuckerberg Initiative. We are living in another era of billionaire-powered philanthropy. And the billionaires shine so brightly, they can tend to block out everyone else.

Including all of us.

We Americans are generally very generous. Globally, the United States comes in at number three in the World Giving Index, which measures giving behaviors such as donating to a charitable organization, helping a stranger, and volunteering time.[2] Indonesia and Kenya lead the way as the most generous countries, with Indonesia ranking first for five years running.

Americans give and volunteer often and a lot. Half of all Americans donate to charitable organizations, and that percentage rises as we age.[3] A quarter of us regularly volunteer our time.[4] In fact, volunteering and giving are more popular activities than watching football (unless it's the Super Bowl) and having sex.[5] In 2023, Americans gave $557 billion charitably. As astonishing as that number is, it's the second year in a row that the dollar amount has decreased.[6]

Even more worrisome, the data also show that more and more giving is being done by the very wealthiest among us. In a year when U.S. charitable giving was down, the wealthiest Americans accounted for 5 percent of all individual giving.[7] Causes for this include economic uncertainty, surging inflation, and record levels of charitable giving the previous two years. Without the contributions of billionaire donors, the apparent shrinking of charitable giving would be even more dramatic.

Part of the context for this data is the yawning and frankly immoral wealth gap. The richest Americans own and control a grossly disproportionate share of wealth. According to the Institute of Taxation and Economic Policy, a nonprofit, nonpartisan tax policy organization, more than $1 in $4 of wealth in the United States is held by the teeny, tiny fraction of the U.S. households with net worths over $30 million (one quarter of 1 percent).[8]

Another piece of context is that the philanthropic sector measures only dollars given to 501(c)(3) charitable organizations, and 501(c)(3) giving accounts for a tiny fraction of all giving by Americans. Giving to individuals, friends, and family, remittances sent to countries of origin (for immigrants), any political sector giving—none of this is counted or included in philanthropic data. This is especially true for people who are *not* part of the wealthiest few percents. If we want to capture a truer picture of generosity, we have to widen our vistas.[9]

The story of philanthropy in the United States has never been fully told. Historically, it has been told as a wealthy person's story, which has usually made it a white story, a man's story, and often, a dead white man's story. But that has never been the full picture.

To understand the full array of American philanthropic practice, we need to open up the aperture. We need to think way bigger than Big Phil. It is by expanding our notions of who is a philanthropist and what counts as philanthropy that we will democratize the field and practice of philanthropy and be able to understand the extent to which money and resources flow throughout our communities. Expanding our idea of who is a philanthropist means including and considering culture—where we come from, what we inherit in terms of cultural legacy, and what we want to pass on to future generations. It also means including groups of people who give together, collective givers and giving circles. Expanding our idea of what counts as philanthropy means including assets beyond money given to charitable organizations, like cash to individuals, political sector giving, remittances sent abroad, volunteer time, and the use of one's voice and networks to influence political and social change.

PHILANTHROPY CONCEIVED IN this broader way is not only for wealthy people; it's by and for all of us.

At its best, philanthropy is not just a sector. It is a component of civil society and one of the most meaningful ways we can show up as citizens who care for one another. In fact, philanthropy is part of the fabric of a functioning and healthy democracy, and ever since "our people"—however you define your people—have been a people, we've always practiced it, often in groups.

We are living in a sociopolitical moment when so many seek to limit access, narrow rights, tighten definitions of who is a citizen, constrict definitions of sexuality and gender, restrict who and where and how one can vote. So much opens up if we can think expansively about who is a citizen, a voter, a lover, a family, and also, who is a donor or philanthropist. The world unfurls, and the possibilities become limitless; more of us can be applied to and called upon to do good.

In the spirit of this expansive mindset, I had the great privilege and good fortune of interviewing over one hundred wealthy people of color across the United States to better understand the scope of philanthropy in communities of color. For me, this journey starts with Urv.

Urvashi Vaid—may she rest in peace and power—was a big expander of many apertures. In a personal and poignant postscript upon her death, Masha Gessen wrote that Urv was "almost certainly, the most prolific LGBTQ organizer in history."[10] There's a famous photo of Urvashi taken in 1990 when she held up a sign in a hotel ballroom where President George H. W. Bush was delivering his first speech on AIDS, ten years into the epidemic. The sign says, "Talk is Cheap. AIDS funding is not." Urv's eyes are trained on the security guard who is about to escort her out of the ballroom. Gessen describes her expression as "a look of unparalleled indignation, a look that would make opponents shrivel and allies fawn."[11]

In addition to being a leader in the fight for LGBTQ+ liberation, Urv was a lawyer, theorist, lifelong activist, and badass. She was also a bass player in a punk rock band, and I like to think that I heard echoes of that in her deep, foundational, rhythmic, down-to-the-bones, unwavering, sometimes howling righteousness. She was a rock star to me before I ever had the great honor to work with her. She scared the crap out of me, until she didn't. She cooked for the people in her circle generously and often, and like me, she was a football fan. She was principled, sometimes uncompromising, intense, and driven by values having to do with the freedom and liberation of all of us.

Urv's seed of an idea many years ago, her question—why weren't there more queer folks and people of color visible in philanthropy?—helped start whole ecosystems. Like many such inspirations, there was a touch of outrage at its core: we know we're *out there*, why the heck aren't we *in here*? She turned her prodigious intellect and drive to raising and moving hundreds of millions of dollars to social-change causes. In the early 1990s, she was a progenitor of OutGiving, which brought gay donors together to fund queer liberation. She wrote in plain and compelling language about the connections between movements, for example, how women's reproductive rights were intimately connected with the rights of gay men to have sex, because both are fundamentally about the power of the state to control our bodies.

In 2015, Urvashi convened a few of us to ask a similar question: where are the wealthy folks of color? We were all women of color and frequent speakers on the philanthropy and social-change circuits. Yet in philanthropic spaces, especially those that brought together wealthy donors, there were virtually no folks of color in any of the rooms we were in. Each of us knew wealthy donors of color personally, yet they were almost always absent in the rooms that convened wealthy people. So Urv led a project that sought to first find them in the philanthropic literature, then second, to find them in real life and share their stories. In 2016, Urv penned a landscape analysis, *The Apparitional Donor*,[12] with Ashindi Maxton, to prove the existence of people of color as donors in the philanthropic literature. I helped do some of the research for the landscape, and while we found a lot, the data were old, pointillistic, and unaggregated, which renders less the sum power of giving by people of color. Further, there was virtually nothing in the literature about wealthy people of color as donors.

In the years following, I worked alongside them and others to build the Donors of Color Network, the nation's first-ever network of wealthy folks of color. The Donors of Color Network was revolutionary because not only had people of color been largely ignored in the philanthropic literature, but they had also not been meaningfully integrated into the networks that bring wealthy people together to do good. The Donors of Color Network is a critical addition to the philanthropic ecosystem in the United States because it provides a philanthropic home for wealthy folks of color, a home that was built by and for them, for us. As we often said when we were building it, let's create the party we want to be at. It's the difference between being in your own home and a perpetual guest at someone else's.

Over two years, I led a qualitative research project that culminated in a report, *Philanthropy Always Sounds Like Someone Else: A Portrait of High Net Wealth Donors of Color*. My small team and I interviewed 150 donors of color across the United States, witnessing, recording, and sharing their stories.[13] One of my first interviews was with an Indian American man who told me about his family's journey to the United States, via Uganda, and how the humble motel they were able to buy became the first stop for dozens of country kin making the same journey. A Vietnamese American woman shared how her family had been helped by U.S. churches and nonprofits when they were escaping the Vietnam War, and how she is now translating Vietnamese cultural norms around reciprocity into her philanthropic practice today, which includes supporting faith-based and refugee organizations. I interviewed an Iranian Cuban punk rocker who directs his family foundation, an African American woman who built a fortune owning McDonald's franchises and whose first foray into philanthropy has been to build a domestic violence shelter, and a Latino small business owner who is finding success in his "second" life after being incarcerated in his early twenties.

Our sample included dozens of "the millionaire next door," regular people whose names you've never heard of who have lived unremarkable yet remarkable lives, accumulated wealth, and are now giving back hundreds of thousands of dollars, if not millions, to their communities. The folks I interviewed are literally changing the face of philanthropy. They expand the idea of who is a philanthropist and what counts as philanthropy. Together, these folks represent a huge opportunity to bring new energy, insights, experiences, and resources to bear at a time in our country's history when this is more important than ever.

In some ways, by interviewing these people often in their own homes, we said to them, "I see you. You are part of the American philanthropic story." We asked them, "What is the bigger 'We' that we might create together?" and we listened. As interviewers and researchers, we could be curious and interested. We could reach across the divides of our personal life experiences, ages, and racial and ethnic identities to ask, listen, witness, then share. As builders, we could build a vehicle (which became known as the Donors of Color Network) to create space for people to come together, across differences, to create something bigger, together. This role of listening, witnessing, and inviting in is a key one when we get to building belonging, building community, and building giving circles.

In one memorable interview, Jorge, a Black professor in his fifties, shared, "As a young child, I was living in a station wagon with my mother, father, and siblings. Doors opened for me while simultaneously shutting for everyone I was in that station wagon with—I was good at school, articulate, a man; I was tall, I could command a room. I was the first male in my family to graduate from high school, and the first person in my family to graduate from college ... My grandmother used to say, 'Service is the rent you pay for living'—a common [saying] in the South—[and that] you cannot be rich and have a poor sister. You help family." Jorge attributes part of his success to an "Auntie Mame"[14] who taught him how to read a restaurant menu and planted the idea in his head that he might go to college. He said of her, "In every king there is a kid, and in every kid there is a king, and she saw both the king and the kid in me." I cry every time I remember that conversation.

Jorge is a deeply philanthropic man. He's also irreverent, sometimes bitingly funny, and a lifelong community-minded activist. He and his partner have adopted several children, mentor literally dozens more, and give away more than $50,000 annually to political and charitable organizations. He referenced two phrases that I heard frequently while I was deep in this oral history research project: "There but for the grace of God go I" and "Service is the price you pay for living."

Nestled in the heart of those two ideas is faith, family, and culture. The legacy of spiritual and faith practices came up in almost all the interviews, across cultural and generational life experiences. Philanthropy and faith have been married since ancient times, so it is unsurprising that faith (including its discontents) was a prominent theme. In fact, I might even say that it would be ahistorical to disentangle faith and philanthropy because faith is, in many ways, part of philanthropy's origin story.

Jandel's story is about expanding what counts as philanthropy. She comes from a rich culture of generosity, baked into her via a beautiful lineage of generous women, none of whom had "two nickels to rub together." Jandel is an African American doctor in her early sixties.[15] She's a quilter and an avid bird watcher. We met in her cheery office, surrounded by bright, whimsical, nature-themed quilts she had made. Jandel told me about her maternal grandmother, the matriarch of the family. For thirty years, her grandmother and her twin sister worked as maids at the fanciest hotel in town. Jandel's grandmother owned her own home, and her sister lived with her. She was very active in the Catholic church, was a member of the Women's Sodality Club, washed and ironed the altar cloths, and baked cookies monthly for the local Catholic charity. She raised six children as a single parent for a large part of her adult life. She was the voter registration block captain and was active in the War on Rats, a community initiative to clean up the neighborhood and end a severe rat infestation. She cooked dinner every Monday night for whichever extended family member could attend, sometimes for as many as twenty people. They called her house "the Ponderosa," after the television show *Bonanza*.

The community-minded spirit rubbed off on Jandel's mom, who was her Girl Scout troop leader, and her aunt, who raised foster children and ran a Catholic summer camp for Black girls. When Jandel's father died, her grandmother came to the house, cooked, took care of the kids, and helped raise them. Jandel says, "Best I can tell, she and her sister were always maids. Every day, she got up, took the bus, and worked."

With tears of deep love, respect, and simply missing her, Jandel described her grandmother: "She had so little, yet she gave so much. I learned generosity from her." Jandel told me, "I come from a family where no one went to college, except for me. I have a sort of survivor guilt. By a ton, I have the highest income, by far, OMG, by a ton." She and her husband earned their wealth by working corporate and medical jobs for decades, building equity in their home, and accumulating retirement accounts and an investment portfolio." Jandel said, "When I was growing up, if you were browner than a paper bag, you were not one of those Blacks. Y'all wouldn't have had any interest in me twenty years ago because I wasn't the right color and my hair wasn't right." Black fraternal and sororal organizations have long and proud legacies of volunteerism and community service, so the couple found other outlets. Jandel does not feel wealthy even though her accountant tells her she is. At the time of our conversation, Jandel and her husband were giving away around $70,000 per year to charitable organizations like their local community foundation, a women's health organization, and a local college, in addition to political causes and candidates, and in support of their family. In Jandel's family, giving is passed down from generation to generation. Her family are community philanthropists who give not only their money but also their time, labor, networks, and heart.

The people I interviewed are all people of color and they're all wealthy. The median annual giving of the people interviewed for *The Portrait* report was $87,500, with folks giving between $5,000 (a young person who was not yet in control of their expected familial wealth) and $17 million annually. Twenty-two percent of this group reported liquid net assets north of $30 million. Apart from a handful of inheritors, none of this sample grew up wealthy. Most grew up working class, poor, and in some cases, very poor. Eighty-eight percent of the people I interviewed helped out their friends and families monetarily, in one case in the form of remittances sent to a home country (this person is an immigrant) in the amount of $2 million per year.

Interviewing wealthy folks of color and getting their stories out into the world emphatically adds them to the story of philanthropy in the United States. There is much more of the potent legacies of generosity in communities of color yet to be unearthed. We have not yet fully appreciated or harvested the bounty and power held in those cultures and cultural practices of generosity, many of which are practiced collectively in communities.

ANOTHER UNDERRECOGNIZED FORM of philanthropy—and one that often thrives in communities of color—takes the form of giving circles and collectives of people doing good together. Generosity is so much more than writing a check, and what's so unpretentiously marvelous about giving circles is that the people in them almost always give away more than their money. When we consider different kinds of giving, I like to think of what many call the Five T's: time, talent, treasure, testimony, and ties. Time is volunteering, and talent might be providing low-bono or pro-bono services like web design or legal advice. Treasure is money, while testimony and ties come into play when we use our voices, networks, and influence to help family, friends, kin, and neighbors.

Your family might have called it tithing, *tzedakah, zakat, tanda, sou sou, i-sou-sou, sols, tam tam, geh, arisan, mahiber,* or mutual aid. These practices are all rooted in culture and they are all practiced in groups. It is by reconnecting with our own cultures of generosity that we can build more meaningful, durable, relevant, and bounteous philanthropic practice today.

• • •

SARA AND LYORD are generous givers who come from deep cultures of giving. Both include giving circles in their philanthropic practices.

Sara Lomelin is a cofounder of the Peninsula Latina Giving Circle. She grew up in Mexico City as part of a large Catholic family. Her parents instilled in their children the idea of service—you work, you take care of your family, and you help your neighbors and larger community. You hear Sara's laugh long before you see her big smile. She describes herself as "that mom," the one who ran the school auction, organized the soccer snacks, and volunteered to be class parent. Her son's friends thought she ran the school.

When Sara immigrated to Texas after marrying, she found a group of other Mexican American women who were pooling their money and sending it to an organization that helped recent immigrants. A few years later, after moving to the Bay Area, a friend connected her to the Latino Community Foundation, and there, she took that idea of pooling money to make change and ran with it. Within a few years, thanks in large part to Sara's cheerleading, coaching, hustling, and organizing, the Latino Community Foundation had created the Latino Giving Circle Network. Today, the Network includes twenty-two giving circles up and down the great state of California, including hers, the Peninsula Latina Giving Circle. In ten years, the network has mobilized more than five hundred individuals in twenty giving circles and, collectively, they've given $2.5 million to over one hundred Latino-led and Latino-serving nonprofits in the state, organizations that do everything from providing direct services for immigrants and refugees and supplying community services for farm working families, to building Latino entrepreneurship, helping families access COVID vaccinations, and much more.

Sara now leads Philanthropy Together, the first-ever organization that supports the burgeoning global giving circle movement. She envisions a more just world powered by everyday givers and sees giving circles as a key way to diversify and democratize philanthropy. I was on the codesign team that helped birth Philanthropy Together, so I'm not exactly unbiased, but I think you'll agree that the work Sara is doing is pretty amazing. Philanthropy Together aims to grow the giving circle movement exponentially over the next five years to include thousands of giving circles mobilizing hundreds of thousands of individuals, moving billions of dollars collectively.[16]

Sara has built upon her Mexican and Catholic traditions of helping neighbors, family, and friends and has exponentially multiplied it by building giving circles around the world, across many communities and cultures similar to and totally different from the one in which she grew up.

Lyord Watson Jr., grew up in Brewton, a small town in southern Alabama, just north of the Florida Panhandle. His mom was a public school teacher for thirty-three years and his dad worked as a laborer at the local paper mill. His family were churchgoers. His dad was a deacon, and Lyord's grandfather was a preacher. He says his dad took his role as deacon very seriously: "It was all about widows and orphans ... He'd get up on Saturday after working the graveyard shift and cut grass, build ramps, just do stuff for folks who needed it. If something needed doing in our community, my family was helping out." Lyord learned generosity by seeing it and living it, organically in his family and community.

What is that goodness, that essential life force that flows through communities like blood through veins? Surely it is not just money. It's people like Lyord's dad, giving with their hands, time, compassion, and advice, lending an ear, and being there for their neighbors.

Lyord's family had always taken up two kinds of offerings at church—offering tithes and a "love offering," to help support the ministry or someone in the community. While he might call this community philanthropy now, his family never used those words to describe what they'd always done. Lyord said he'd never heard the word *philanthropy* until he joined the Birmingham Change Fund, a local giving circle that's now nearly twenty years old.

Lyord was introduced to the Birmingham Change Fund by a friend named Charles Lewis. As soon as he learned about the organization, he was moved by the idea of helping Black communities, together with other Black folks, in Birmingham and its environs.

In the same way that his parents had brought up their offerings in church each week, Lyord attended giving circle meetings, began to make financial contributions, and volunteered his talents and time. As time went by, he became more and more involved, and in 2013, Lyord was one of two members of the Birmingham Change Fund who ran for the local school board. They both won and served from 2013 to 2017. Following the example of his father, Lyord kept on asking—who needs help and how can we help them? In this way, he kept on learning and kept on pushing upstream. He told me, "There are symptoms and there are issues. Often, people want to fund symptoms and don't want to deal with root issues. Like let's say a student is behind in reading—so we fund reading. But what are the reasons that kid is behind in reading in the first place? What's going on at home? Is the kid hungry? The schools that are in higher-income neighborhoods tend to do better than the schools in the lower-than-average-median-income areas. There's a connection between healthcare, socioeconomics, and education. If you can solve the socioeconomic issue, you can solve education and health. You might solve some other stuff, too."

Another issue Lyord is working on is funding for Black businesses, and for this, his inspiration is William Reuben Pettiford, a minister and banker who started the Alabama Penny Savings Bank in 1890 by pooling money from Black churches to make loans. Inspired by Pettiford's model, Lyord created the Penny Foundation to fund the development of Black Birmingham. The Penny Foundation makes microgrants to small businesses to help them grow. One man, an electrician, borrowed $1,000 to buy a piece of equipment that helped him attract commercial clients. Lyord told me, "I cannot get that man to come to my house now because he's teaching at the Mercedes plant. His business has boomed because of that $1,000 microgrant." This year, the Penny Foundation hopes to give grants amounting to $2.5 million.

Lyord draws a direct line from his churchgoing family roots to joining a giving circle to running for the local school board to his work today, which reckons with the racial wealth gap by building Black community ownership and wealth. For many of us thinking about philanthropy, the question we ask is, "How can I help?" but Lyord provides an inspiring example of how the most effective helpers also dig deeper. Rather than simply redirecting resources, he's gone one step upstream each time, always asking, "But why?"—with each step firmly grounded in the underpinnings of his cultural heritage. The best giving circles create space for members to both address direct needs and also think about core underlying issues.

They wouldn't necessarily describe themselves this way, but Sara and Lyord are the living members of ancient families and peoples. Their people came from continents away and have survived the Middle Passage and enslavement; centuries of racism, xenophobia, and colonialism; famine, war, and economic hardship.

Even though they are doing something from time immemorial and reconnecting with their heritages, Sara and Lyord are building a new framework for expressing their values in the world. By joining with others to make a difference in their communities, they redefine philanthropic practice to be about more than an individual. They are centering the We over a Me. They are at once drawing from their pasts and building into their futures, connecting within and across communities and backgrounds in order to do good with others. Collective giving and giving circles are meaningful vehicles to carry their philanthropic work forward.

I'M ON A LIVELY LISTSERV of philanthropy professionals, people who work in foundations, do research on the sector, think about charitable infrastructure, and the like. The 2023 annual Giving USA report had just come out in June 2023 (sharing data for 2022), citing some of the figures I shared earlier, that charitable giving by individuals had gone down in the United States, that levels of participation were down, that technology-enabled giving is up yet giving is down, that if it weren't for the billionaires, the story would be even more bleak. There was a flurry of fret and worry over this "crisis" in charitable giving. Billionaires are individuals, too, so they "count" as individual givers, but for this group, it was worrisome that nonbillionaire giving seemed to be on the decline.

Coincidentally, that same week I'd spoken with Rafa. He's a musician who lives in the Boston area. His family is from the Dominican Republic. Rafa's dad has been part of a Dominican "*san*" for twenty years and it is going strong. The *san* is a group of twenty or so people who put a couple hundred dollars into it every week. The group communicates via WhatsApp and it is run by a woman named Carmen. She keeps the spreadsheet, organizes the lottery to determine in what order people will get their money, and she texts reminders to all in the *san*, "Hey, it's Thursday, reminder to send the Zelle or CashApp today."

Like many of these informal, shared, collective efforts, this one is under the radar. I asked Rafa if I might speak with Carmen and he said, "um, no."

IN 2008, Rafa's family lost everything, and it was tough to make ends meet. One of the things that helped them stay afloat was his dad's participation in multiple *sans*. He puts money in every week, and over a three- or four-month period, his turn will come up and he'll receive $4,000 or $5,000. For his family, the *sans* helped bridge the gap. Rather than feeling alone during their family's financial crisis, they were connected with others. As Rafa told me, "America is so 'dog eat dog' with this shit . . . *sans* are a way of pulling up and making sure we're *all* okay."

Rafa has participated a few times when he and his partner can afford it. He got his turn last November, and he said with a grin, "It felt great. Yup. I earned that." It's all word of mouth, friends of friends, and in Rafa's dad's case, the people in the *san* often come from the same region of the Dominican Republic. Rafa has never heard of anyone running away or cheating. Occasionally someone needs a day or two to come up with their share, but they work it out with Carmen. His mom isn't crazy about it because "he's constantly paying and they're often short," but the money flows back around. Plus, she occasionally joins a *sou sou*!

From the point of view of Rafa's dad's *san*, there is no charitable crisis in the United States. There might very well be an affordability crisis, but there is no generosity crisis here. There is only a group of loosely yet deeply connected people who pool money to help bridge gaps and build community.

The crisis in modern philanthropy has to do with everyday Americans feeling lonely, like they can't effect change, and feeling disconnected from each other and from their communities. The crisis has to do with Big Phil—the overindexing of billionaire philanthropy and all the extraneous structures, measurements, and metrics it has created to prioritize and justify itself.

THERE IS A CRISIS in philanthropy, but it's not what this group of philanthropy professionals was fretting about. Their crisis happens only when you look at the narrow slice of generosity practice that philanthropy professionals consider. To get a fuller picture, we've got to count *sans, gehs, tandas, sou sous*, remittances, giving circles, direct giving to individuals, political giving, volunteering, and values-aligned investing. To appreciate the full bounty of American philanthropic practice, we've got to think way past any individual, even a very rich one, toward an expansive notion of who is a philanthropist and what counts as philanthropy.

3

RIP, Big Phil

If Big Phil had a spiritual and intellectual home, it would be Stanford University, nestled in Silicon Valley where so many of its fortunes were made. Stanford is the home of the Stanford Social Innovation Review, one of the major publications in the philanthropy/social innovation industry, and of the Stanford Center on Philanthropy and Civil Society (commonly referred to as Stanford PACS). And if Big Phil had a professor emeritus, it would be Paul Brest.

Paul Brest is a legend. He's the former head of the William and Flora Hewlett Foundation and cofounder of Stanford PACS. There's a building named after him at Stanford Law School. Paul is the major evangelist for "strategic philanthropy," and his book *Money Well Spent* is its manifesto.

Paul had been an important early advisor to Jeff and Tricia Raikes, the founders of the Raikes Foundation. For several years now, I've been part of a philanthropy collaborative that was started by the Raikes Foundation. It began as a smallish group of foundation, academic, consultant, donor network types who were all working with wealthy to very wealthy people to move more money, faster, toward "impact."

Paul and I were both members of this philanthropy collaborative. He was the professorial lion in the room, and I the Midwestern, Korean American "nobody special." I was there as a newbie to the wealthy philanthropy world, having worked mostly on the (less rich) nonprofit and giving circle areas of the sector. I was part of a team doing the research that would eventually lead to the birth of the Donors of Color Network, and I'd been invited to join the collaborative because #PhilanthropySoWhite. I was new to that kind of space and felt particularly confused about the terms; I remember plaintively asking, day one, why there was this ivory-tower hyperfocus on "impact" and "strategy" when I'd never known a nonprofit person or organizational leader who was not strategic or who didn't want to have impact. The words seemed kind of obvious. It was September 2019 and we were meeting in person in a beautiful, windowed room that overlooked one of Seattle's many lakes.

Paul and I frequently disagreed. At this one meeting, Paul was expounding on the primacy of metrics, evaluation, and donor intent, seeming to make an argument that values don't matter, that "good" philanthropy should be values-neutral because "good" philanthropy benefits people equally. I asked him for examples of philanthropy that were values-neutral. He said that funding for medical research is an example of philanthropy that is unprejudiced by the application of any values, that benefits everyone equally. I replied with a list: Henrietta Lacks, the infamous Tuskegee experiments on Black men, the fact that women are underrepresented in medical research and clinical trials, that Black women especially are underrepresented and underserved, the fact that health outcomes for women of color are worse than for white women. Anyone would be hard-pressed to identify an arena that is untainted by history, societal systems, the application of values, wittingly or not. I remember his eyes bulged as he practically spat at me, "Well, Hali, perhaps you don't belong in this room."

Paul could not tolerate me coexisting with him in his professional space, a space he was used to owning. He was blind to his own prejudice because of the insularity of his privilege.

Later, at a staff debrief attended only by Raikes Foundation staff and consultants, someone asked if anyone had heard what Paul had said to me. Not a single person had. Thank god the person had brought it up, otherwise it would've been as if a tree had fallen in the forest and no one had seen it crush an Asian American woman on its way down.

This incident has stayed with me. There were only three other women of color in the collaborative and that meeting is seared into our memories. We bonded then and have remained colleagues and friends today. The four of us were brand-new to the collaborative. The white women at the table, all of whom had way more tenure than we did, said nothing and were completely silent. They didn't come to my aid, nor did they say anything to me after.

Incidentally, choosing silence over support is what causes fractures instead of solidarity. Think back to the early days of the suffragette movement when white women leaders made a deliberate choice to separate themselves from Black women leaders (who had labored alongside them until that point), setting back the cause of Black voting rights and fracturing the fight for gender equality that continues to this day. As Esther Armah, author of *Emotional Justice*, said at Omega Institute recently, "We cannot always summon courage, but we really should be able to always summon support."[1]

Paul Brest's way of thinking about philanthropy—prioritizing donor intent while applying technocratic, business-minded, experts-know-best means, has been the predominant frame for the past twenty years. I've never liked it. I've labored under it, jumped through many hoops to satisfy it, and now I am trying my best to get our sector to appreciate it, retain its good parts, and move on.

If you work in the nonprofit or philanthropy sector and have been mystified, buried under, or hurled things across the room because of logic models, KPIs (key performance indicators), or metrics that don't seem to apply to anything that matters to you, you can thank strategic philanthropy. Along with Stanford PACS, the Bill & Melinda Gates Foundation and the Robin Hood Foundation in New York City are well-known (and very well-funded by business leaders) proponents of this style of giving.

Strategic philanthropy has been criticized for prioritizing top-down, ivory-tower strategists (and the donors who fund them) who too often disregard the firsthand knowledge of people doing the work. In fact, Brest's coauthor, Hal Harvey, wrote an apology in *The Chronicle of Philanthropy* in 2016 titled "Why I Regret Pushing Strategic Philanthropy" based on his own experience with arrogant funders who thought they knew best and who made him conform to overly precise strategies and rigid accountability structures.

Applying business models to social change efforts has always felt like cramming novels onto spreadsheets. Spreadsheets can tell a story, but not the full one. And novels are better than spreadsheets for matters having to do with human dignity, belonging, joy, suffering, faith, justice, fairness, courage, and hope.

Like many sectors, philanthropy is reckoning with power. From the sector's earliest days, thoughtful practitioners, including Andrew Carnegie, have considered its inherent tensions. In *The Gospel of Wealth*, Carnegie wrote about the inevitable caste system that arises with extreme wealth inequality, and how the very wealthy have a moral obligation to give away their money in order to lessen that inequality. The very business of one party giving away money and another party receiving it to do good is already a system rife with imbalances of power.

Fundamentally, to not listen deeply to communities most affected, to not consider history, race, and the economic and social systems in which some groups have been privileged over others is to choose to operate with blinders on. No matter how perfectly neat and tidy your logic model, metrics evaluation, or theory of change are, race, history, gender, culture, and economic and social systems will blur, complicate, enliven, and enrich every time.

In some ways, the emergence of ideas like proximity, community-led solutions, and giving circles are a power-focused correction from the previously dominant frame. At the time of our lakeside showdown, strategic philanthropy was being challenged by numerous community-minded upstarts including Trust-Based Philanthropy, Collective Giving, Community-centric philanthropy, and others.[2] Like most things, strategic philanthropy is not all bad, but it exerted outsize influence because of its outsize backers. It's now time for it to take its place among many other valid philanthropic frames.

. . .

IF STRATEGIC PHILANTHROPY is like cramming novels into spreadsheets, effective altruism is like ditching the novels altogether. Effective altruism (EA) is a philosophy and philanthropic movement that strictly applies data and logic to the goal of ending human suffering. EA is inspired by the philosopher Peter Singer who, alongside others in the utilitarian ethical tradition, is concerned with maximizing good outcomes and minimizing bad outcomes. For effective altruists, this entails rigorous research into maximal philanthropic efficiency—if $10 spent on mosquito nets prevents five cases of malaria and saves two lives, and $10 toward a local charity helping single mothers saves zero lives, so much the worse for single mothers (or so the effective altruist might say).

There's a logic to EA. Why waste money, time, and resources when you can avoid it? Why not make use of all the data and computing power available to us to make efficient philanthropic decisions? EA takes this logic to its extreme. If you want to help animals, it's generally more impactful (in terms of tangible, measurable impact) to get rich and donate money than to volunteer at a shelter. So, an effective altruist would say that's what you should do. Unfortunately, according to their data, it's almost always more efficient to earn and then donate money rather than directly involve yourself with this or that cause. So off to Wall Street and Silicon Valley they go.

EA also tends to get caught up in issues that many of us would find bizarre. Since we, as hypothetical effective altruists, want to maximize human pleasure, doesn't that mean we want to maximize the number of happy humans? This is the type of question asked by the "longtermists" within EA, who alongside considering potential existential risks to humanity (especially the risk of an AI apocalypse, one of their primary pet concerns), focus a lot of energy on maximizing the number of happy future people. They do this through encouraging high birth rates among the smart and successful, alongside other practices that, to an outside observer, might begin to resemble something like eugenics.

Unfortunately, the parallels between eugenic thinking and philanthropy are deeply rooted. Andrew Carnegie, that scion and member of the other Gilded Age in America, was profoundly influenced by the English philosopher Herbert Spencer, who pioneered Social Darwinism. Spencer argued that those who rose to the top were naturally the best; the phrase *survival of the fittest* is his, not Charles Darwin's. In the pre-Industrial "barbarian" age, the physically strongest men flourished. After the Industrial Revolution, it would be the cleverest and most hardworking men who would thrive. He counseled that helping poor people interferes with natural selection because people needed to compete for resources if society, and the human race, were to advance. "Without struggle, there is no progress," he wrote. Of the disabled, Spencer opined, "it is best they should die."[3] Carnegie and other industrial giants of his generation found in Spencer justification for their success. John D. Rockefeller wrote, "There is no evil tendency in business, merely the working out of a law of nature and a law of God."[4] For both EA adherents today and the robber barons of the late nineteenth and early twentieth centuries, a higher calling ends up justifying some pretty horrifying beliefs.

In many ways, EA is the apotheosis, the natural child, of the logic of strategic philanthropy. Once humans have been reduced to data points, it can begin to seem reasonable to plug them into all sorts of calculations. Each present person is worth one point, and each future person is worth one point, so a policy that harms a thousand today to benefit a million in a hundred years? That's an easy choice for an effective altruist. Spend $1,000 on your child's medical bills or $1,000 on ten children's medical bills somewhere across the world? Another easy choice. Kinship, justice, faith, culture—these are some of the things worth zero points in the EA calculus.

EA has taken root in Silicon Valley, and among its more infamous boosters is Sam Bankman-Fried, the crypto whiz kid who was sentenced to twenty-five years in prison for stealing billions from customers. EA's proponents tend to be young men, and it is particularly popular among tech and finance bros. Its three main tenets are (1) make a lot of money so you can donate a lot of money, (2) do the most good for the most people, and (3) do intense evaluations to figure out the most effective way to help the most people, then follow rigorously the logic of those evaluations.

The absence of a sense of equity, fairness, culture, values, or justice can lead to problematic logical ends. As my daughter, Maya (a PhD candidate in philosophy at CUNY, City University of New York) explained to me, "If killing Nicholas [her partner] will result in saving ten more lives, they don't care that it sucks for me to have to kill Nicholas, or that he dies."

LUCKILY THERE ARE people in the philanthropy world who have evolved the other direction, toward humanity rather than away from it. Jeff and Tricia Raikes started their philanthropic journey in the bosom of Stanford University (he's an alum and was on their board of directors). Paul Brest was an early teacher, mentor, and guide. But from that business-minded, technocratic, top-down, metrics-over-everything frame, their philanthropic strategy has evolved toward complexity and systems frames, and their mindset has evolved alongside, too, toward listening, humility, and deep respect for community.

Jeff and Tricia were early employees at Microsoft; they met there and were the first Microsoft couple to get married. Neither grew up wealthy. Tricia grew up working class in Seattle; her mom was the church secretary. Jeff grew up on a farm in Nebraska. To this day, his happy place is sitting on a tractor. Jeff led the business division at Microsoft, retiring after twenty-seven years to become the first CEO of the Bill & Melinda Gates Foundation. Jeff and Tricia started the Raikes Foundation twenty years ago with an initial influx of $109 million, and as of February 2024, it had distributed $201 million to charitable causes. The foundation gives away around $19 million a year to two primary funding areas: Youth-Serving Systems (education and housing stability for youth) and Resourcing Equity and Democracy. Raikes is a "spend down foundation," meaning the couple intend to spend down its assets (and a significant portion of their own personal assets as well) before they die. Like many wealthy families, the couple also give through other vehicles like DAFs, and via their family office.

Education is one of the Raikes Foundation's priorities. Early on in their education learning journey, they focused on the kids—youth and adolescent brain development, good sleep, nutrition, self-esteem, antibullying, critical thinking (all important and worthy)—and on the teachers who teach them, which meant teacher training and standardized test scores.

As the couple dove deeper into issues in education, they kept asking, "But why?" Why are there so many children in Seattle's schools who are missing school, who need services for housing, who aren't being well served by the school system, who need remediation, who are hungry, who are basically showing up symptomatic of many of the social ills faced by Seattle generally?

And quickly, Tricia shared, they had an important insight: "Kids aren't messed up. Systems are."

There's a parable about babies in the water. It's sometimes told as two people walking along a riverbank when they notice babies floating by on the river. One of them jumps in and starts grabbing babies out of the water. The other runs upstream. The first yells at the second, "Hey! Where are you going? Help me save these babies!" And the second replies, "I'm going to see who's throwing babies in the water!"

Obviously, we need *both* the baby savers and the ones running upstream to figure out how those babies are ending up in the river in the first place! And making deep social change in communities is a lot more complicated than the false binary of either saving babies or running upstream. As it relates to the philanthropy folks who are metrics-obsessed, it is a lot easier to count babies saved than it is to count and measure the more "upstream" interventions, which tend to be systemic and intertwined. It's also easier to reward baby savers with philanthropic dollars (in the form of grants and donations) because that more downstream intervention is easier to count and an easier story to tell (akin to reporting that X number of meals were delivered, X number of seniors served, X number of kids attended this camp, etc.).

I heard Angelique Power, CEO of the Skillman Foundation, speak a few years ago in Detroit. The Skillman Foundation focuses their funding and efforts on behalf of Detroit's youth and the city's education system. Detroit is a very young town, with a median age of thirty-five, and it's a majority Black and Brown city. Gen Z'ers (born 1997 to 2012) are the largest generation, and they also make up a third of the world population, and a quarter of the U.S. population. Angelique said, "They're the most diverse generation of Americans—48 percent are folks of color. One in five are LGBTQ+. One in three know someone who is nonbinary. They're shaped by online connectivity, the pandemic, shootings, racial and political strife. They are optimistic. They feel agency. They were the babies from the banks of the river. And now they are leading us all to a new place, this hopeful, collective us. In this tenuous life, I'm going to spend the rest of my days moving barriers out of their way."[5]

Jeff and Tricia moved upstream from individual kids and teachers toward environments and systems, which includes thinking about what barriers they can remove for the next generation. Their education portfolio is now embedded within a body of work called "Youth-Serving Systems," which also includes housing stability for youth. On their website,[6] they write, "All students deserve educational experiences that affirm who they are and prepare them to thrive. We support youth, educators, and policymakers to reimagine and redesign our public school system so that all young people have an excellent education, no matter who they are or where they live."

The couple dove (and are still diving) deeply and courageously into their own blind spots around race and privilege. They've been part of a "brain trust" of colleagues that includes Darren Walker, the head of the Ford Foundation; Rashad Robinson, head of Color of Change; Marc Morial, head of the Urban League; and Michele Norris, head of the Race Card Project.[7] They're not leaning too hard on executive directors and organizers who run community-based organizations, seeking other funders and peers to be among their learning community instead. When they invite leaders to annual retreats and other learning opportunities, they compensate them (I've been one of those folks and have received funding from the Raikes Foundation). I've been in pretty fractious rooms where a lot of criticism is being directed at donors and philanthropy, and I've observed Jeff and Tricia sitting there, taking notes, just listening. They see themselves as lifelong learners and, more importantly, they have a lot of empathy.

Recently, the Raikes are turning much of their attention toward influencing their wealthy peers, which to my mind is one of the most important things very wealthy people can do because it's one of the few things that *only they* can do. Jeff and Tricia are also convening people across organizations so that entire ecosystems can build relationships, grow, and learn together.[8] Jeff and Tricia are very wealthy, and they are strategically using their access to other wealthy people to influence and move them toward giving more equitably, more upstream, with a more community-centered mindset. They are using their privileged perch in a way that serves the city, communities, and organizations they care about. And they're doing their best to bring along other very wealthy people to do the same.

FAITH-BASED PHILANTHROPY EXISTS at the other end of the ego spectrum than some of the billionaire, "I alone can do this" philanthropists. One of the five pillars of Islam is to give charitably, and public displays of giving are discouraged. The Quran emphasizes the importance of sincerity and humility, and according to a saying by the Prophet Muhammad, one of the seven people granted shade on Judgment Day will be the person who gives charity in secret, without even letting his left hand know what his right hand has given. Judaism holds anonymous giving as among the highest forms of charity. Matthew, Jesus's apostle, and Maimonedes, a twelfth-century Jewish rabbi and philosopher, exhorted both Christians and Jews to maintain the dignity of the poor by remaining anonymous. From the Gospel of Matthew in the New Testament (6:3), which is part of the Sermon on the Mount, "When thou doest alms, let not they left hand know what thy right hand doeth."

The highest ideals of Jewish, Muslim, Christian, and other faiths demand that one give anonymously, which is to remove the self from the philanthropic story completely. It is truly a loss of the ego and the self in service of a higher ideal. But here on earth, there are plenty of monuments to individual, familial, even dynastic wealth in the form of temples, churches, and synagogues with donors' names prominently displayed.

The ideal of the total loss of self is a high bar. Another way to look at this is to ask, Who is the protagonist of this story? Is it me, the donor? Is it that organizational leader over there? Or the charismatic leader over here? Or the volunteer who shows up week over week? Or is it more truthfully the folks on the ground doing the actual hard, courageous work, day after day, year over year? To me, donors, the organization, and its leaders all play an important role. But the star of the show, the thing we ought to keep front of mind, is the *why* we're all in this work in the first place—the mission and vision that benefits a community. The star of the show, the thing to keep front and center, is the collective, all of us.

It's time for Big Phil to Retire In Peace, so other philanthropic frameworks can get more sunlight. Big Phil has had a great run, starting with Andrew Carnegie and continuing up through today with Bill Gates, Mark Zuckerberg, and some of the others you've met in this book so far. He has done a lot of good, including building scores of public libraries and vaccinating millions of children and saving their lives. But measured against making progress on the biggest problems as identified by the UN, Big Phil hasn't made a dent. Big Phil has made billions and given away billions. He has also stashed, stored, and hoarded billions. He almost for sure has not paid his fair share in taxes. Big Phil has hired thousands of people to do good in his name. He has created a complicated myriad of reporting, evaluative, and programmatic forms and structures. He has endowed institutions to research and promulgate his strategic frameworks. He has built great edifices, including foundations, to do the same.

Part of the harm that philanthropy has unwittingly caused by putting donors front and center could be ameliorated by reprioritizing the why over the "I." In some ways, philanthropy is at a fork in the road. Do we want to organize our Five T's to be in service to Big Phil? Or do we want to organize our Five T's, including our money, to be in service to a more people-powered form?

Collective giving is a people-powered form. People who give together are already mixing in some We with the Me, and by pooling our time, talent, treasure, testimony, and ties, everyday donors can have an outsize impact, together.

Thank you for your work, Phil. But you alone cannot save us or our planet.

We need and deserve a more collective response.

Part II

WE

We're Lonely, and the Antidote to Loneliness Is One Another

Philanthropy as it's practiced today has lost the thread. Somewhere along the way, we've relegated the human beings who ought to be center stage off to the wings, replaced by logic models, performance indicators, and so many spreadsheets. Somehow, we've lost our humanity, the yearning to belong, to have efficacy, love, opportunity, and dignity. We've lost the connections to our own cultural roots of generosity, community care, and giving back. We've lost the relationships and connections with one another.

Perhaps unsurprisingly, our society is also in an epidemic of loneliness. Dr. Vivek Murthy, the surgeon general of the United States, released a report in 2023, *Our Epidemic of Loneliness and Isolation: The U.S. Surgeon General's Advisory on the Healing Effects of Social Connection and Community.*[1] Most Americans now report that they're lonely based on a widely used scale that asks questions like, "Do you lack companionship?" or "Do you ever feel left out?"[2]

There are many reasons so many Americans are lonely and literally dying deaths of despair, among them the loss of civic spaces, civic clubs, decreasing participation in faith and other fraternal/sororal communities, and, I would add, our country's relentless worshipping of individualism. Big Phil isn't exactly Ebenezer Scrooge, the protagonist of Charles Dickens's novella *A Christmas Carol*, but he, too, can set himself apart on purpose. In one of the all-time great descriptions of an unhappy, lonely, old miser, Scrooge is described as "a squeezing, wrenching, grasping, scraping, clutching, covetous, old sinner! Hard and sharp as flint ... secret, and self-contained, and solitary as an oyster."[3] Scrooge hates Christmas (a wasteful holiday for spendthrifts) but one fateful Christmas Eve, he is visited by the Ghosts of Christmas Past, Present, and Future and is reborn as a charitable, generous, happier, more socially connected man.

Robert Putnam, Harvard political scientist and author of *Bowling Alone: The Collapse and Revival of American Community*, has been writing for decades about the rise in social isolation and how bad it is for all of us. Since the 1970s, there's been a precipitous decline in community groups like the Elks, the Rotary, the Masons, the Boy Scouts and Girl Scouts, parent-teacher associations, local chapters of political parties, religious institutions, softball teams, union locals, town bands—plus people vote less, host fewer dinner parties, and are more likely to have unlisted phone numbers.[4] Churches, social clubs, men's clubs, women's associations, bridge clubs, and bowling leagues have all dipped in membership and participation. Traditional community groups and organizations have all but faded. We have Instagram and social media, and many of us live in densely populated cities in densely populated neighborhoods and high-rises, yet we feel and are more alone than ever. Humans are an intensely social species, yet we've lost the social thread. And this isolation takes a toll. Loneliness is as deadly as smoking fifteen cigarettes a day, and more lethal than drinking six alcoholic drinks a day.[5]

Nicholas Kristof has been writing a moving series on deaths of despair, inspired by what has happened to some of his childhood classmates with whom he rode the number 6 school bus in rural Yamhill County, Oregon.[6] Today, about one-quarter of the kids who rode the bus with Kristof are dead, and they've died from drugs and alcohol, accidents, and suicides.

Moving from Me to We has an internal psychic aspect and an external social or material one. In Kristof's series, we see how loneliness can drive its sufferers toward substance abuse, depression, and an untimely death. But with some social supports, loneliness can also direct people to find each other. The cures for loneliness are psychic (like meditation, praying, or therapy) and material (finding and joining a group). For the sake of our health and happiness, we just might need more of each other.

Belonging is the antidote to loneliness, and giving circles, doing good in a group, are a great way to build belonging, engagement, and community. They add purpose, doing good together, and money to other groups that you might already belong to.

In fact, many giving circles start with groups that already exist, like a book group; adult soccer team; choir or knitting circle; mutual aid group; parenting, meditation, or dinner group; poker or mah-jong or movie-night group. They naturally exist in their ecosystems, unlike the hired consultants who swooped into Newark to "save" the public school system. Or the team of brilliant technocrats who come in with solutions baked in some faraway oven with no local ingredients. It's hard (not impossible, but hard) to build belonging when you have little in common with the people you're swooping in on.

Though these social groups might naturally exist, there is something very potent about adding conversations about shared values and money into the mix. These added elements deepen the pre-existing relationships, adding in difficult conversations and vulnerabilities. Over time, the bonds strengthen into a committed collective.

Giving circles are not the only way to build belonging, but they're a really good way, and something any of us can do. You don't need to be wealthy to practice generosity (and building community) in this manner. Giving circles bring philanthropic practitioners closer to their communities and the people who inhabit them. Giving circles encourage the type of connection and closeness that Big Phil seems to try to keep at a remove. And giving circles can help knit us back together again.

ACCORDING TO PUBLIC health researchers, social isolation is "the rare malady whose cure is fully known and costs relatively little yet is still so difficult to achieve."[7] The remedies aren't expensive or high-tech. Some of the strategies are as simple as getting people back into such quotidian habits as eating meals together, volunteering to help one another out, and holding parties. The solutions don't require lots of money or individual heroic actions.

Mayors around the world recognize that reconnecting with one another is directly tied to the health of their local democracies. Cities like Helsinki, Finland; Cork, Ireland; Vancouver, Canada; Dakar, Senegal; and Barcelona, Spain, are experimenting with embedding hyperlocality and community building into their urban planning. City officials throughout Sweden have placed moveable furniture in parks and have recorded a 400 percent increase in the amount of time people spend outside in cities, including Stockholm. In June 2023, UN-Habitat, which focuses on sustainable urban development, described this hyperlocal approach as a "key enabler capable of fostering human well-being and effective climate action."[8]

"Conviviality is an economic actor," says Patrick Bernard, a journalist who convened the Republic of Super Neighbors that knits together a roughly fifty-street section of the fourteenth arrondissement in Paris, a mostly residential district on the Seine's Left Bank. He thinks that by encouraging residents to become emotionally and physically invested in the public spaces they live in, they'll be less likely to litter or drop cigarette butts. The group collaborated with a nonprofit to install compost bins across the neighborhood. The bins are used by eight hundred Super Neighbors who process sixty tons of organic waste annually, and an abnormally high 98 percent of that waste gets deposited correctly.[9] How's that for civic engagement! These are great examples of a systems response to what might seem to be a problem of individuals, loneliness.

Forming kinship and being in community with one another helps us all become better citizens. It's much easier to care about a community when you feel you are a part of it. Even loose ties can help connect us with each other. Loose ties can turn into deeper ties if we're open to the possibilities inherent in our neighborhoods, friend groups, and workplaces.

Loose ties are those casual, infrequent, fleeting connections of the type that might happen between neighbors, or with a barista, yoga classmate, mail carrier, bodega cashier, or other dog owners in the park. Loose ties are opportunities for new inputs from slightly different points of view on the same social scene. They are opportunities for new information from people near us, but beyond our more intimate circles; and because the perspective is slightly different than ours, insights bubble. They can be captivating, novel, and might even spark a creative "aha!" Steve Jobs famously designed the Pixar building with a giant lobby/crosswalk/plaza space through which people have to traverse multiple times a day. Not only does it get people up and moving, but the space also invites chance encounters—bumping into someone—with the hopes that coffees will be shared and inspirations kindled.[10]

The idea of loose ties was first promulgated by a researcher at Stanford who looked at how people found and got jobs (loose ties helped more than close ones).[11] For new ideas and inspiration, weak ties were more important than close ones. Loose ties could turn into actual business connections and networks. And the more loose connections we have, the better. A 2016 study connected loose ties to happiness. People with larger networks of acquaintances tend to be happier overall, and have a greater sense of belonging and even of security. Being recognized and feeling connected, even loosely, boosts our mental well-being.[12]

My husband, Peter, and I used to live in Kansas City, and it was our warm-weather custom to take a walk after dinner. Kansas City has long, languorous summer evenings, and our neighborhood had big trees and loud cicadas. We had this chubby little cat named Pookie who walked with us, not on a leash, doing her semiferal thing but always keeping an eye on us nearby. We passed neighbors on their porches and stopped to exchange greetings and news with Dan and Nancy, or Tripp and Di, or Sonya and Dave. It was casual, low-stakes, neighborly, and so, so, *so* pleasant.

Nicholas Kristof writes, "Solutions to loneliness are like that—little nudges to encourage us to mingle the way we evolved to."[13] Beyond exchanging pleasantries, fostering loose ties with neighbors and colleagues is also a way to stay informed about someone's new job, an ill parent, a new teacher at the local school, or a local issue that is starting to percolate. Loose ties can turn into something deeper if we're open to it.

CHURCHES, TEMPLES, AND SYNAGOGUES used to function as town squares. They were the regular, central meeting spots for worship, gossip, and interacting with one another. They have also been the site for weekly alms, donations, offerings, and tithes, which is why philanthropy and faith communities have always been so interconnected. Americans' participation in faith communities has been falling steadily and dramatically, and we are increasingly wary of institutions of all kinds.[14] Jessica Grose wrote a five-part series for the *New York Times* on this decline, and thousands of readers engaged with her about their own heartache at losing the fellowship and community they used to get from their faith communities. Readers wrote about leaving church communities because they'd divorced, or had children out of wedlock, or were gay. But they miss the wraparound social fabric and connection that their places of worship provided. She interviewed sociologists and asked whether secular communities could provide a simulacrum, and the answer was always no. Phil Zuckerman, a professor of sociology and secular studies at Pitzer College, told her: "I can go play soccer on a Sunday morning and hang out with people from different races and different class backgrounds, and we can bond. But I'm not doing that with my grandparents and my grandchildren ... A soccer team can't provide spiritual solace in the face of death, it probably doesn't have a weekly charitable call, and there's no sense of connection to a heritage that goes back generations. You can get bits and pieces of these disparate qualities elsewhere, but there's no 'one-stop shop'— at least not right now."[15]

Grose also interviewed a thirty-six-year-old man who lives in Arizona who had written to her about missing the general sense of community he got from going to church: "Being socially atomized is hard on the spirit." He shared a story that illustrates organized religion at its best. During a section of the service where the pastor asked for "prayers for the people," another congregant, a young man in his early twenties who'd just had a baby and lost his job, asked if the congregation would pray for him. An older man went up to the younger one at the conclusion of the service and offered him a job: "You can come work for me tomorrow." She writes that while that may sound like a Frank Capra movie, church remains one of the few places where people from all walks of life can interact with one another and even help one another.[16]

Obviously, a lot of harm has been done in the name of religion. People have lost their faith in places of worship because, often, those places have lost their faith in them, particularly if they haven't lived life in the "ordained" fashion.

Rabbi Sharon Brous leads a Jewish faith community in Los Angeles, and wrote a book called *The Amen Effect: Ancient Wisdom to Mend Our Broken Hearts and World.*[17] Rabbi Brous makes the case that it is through authentic, human relatedness with each other that we will reconnect with our shared humanity and begin to heal. In fact, it is finding each other in celebration, pain, suffering, vulnerability, and possibility that is the spiritual work of our time. The word *amen* captures this spiritual showing up for each other, affirming via this ancient idea and word, "I see you. You are not alone."

Rabbi Brous describes an ancient pilgrimage during which thousands of Jews would travel to Jerusalem to climb the steps of the Temple Mount, enter its huge plaza, then, all together, turn right and walk counterclockwise. Except for those who were ill, lonely, brokenhearted, or in mourning—these folks would turn left, walking clockwise, always against the current. When someone passed a person in pain, it was customary to look them in the eyes and ask, "What happened to you? Why does your heart ache?" The sad person might answer that a parent had died, and words had been left unsaid, or that a child is sick and they are in need of prayers. The asking person would then respond with a blessing, or words to the effect, "you are not alone." The ancients knew that it could be them, each of us, walking the path of anguish, and that next year, it might be you. Rabbi Brous finds modern lessons in this ancient wisdom. One is, don't suffer alone; reach out. And if you're not suffering, go to the plaza anyway and be that holder and seer for someone else. "'Tell me about your sorrow' may be the deepest affirmation of our humanity, even in terribly inhumane times." This profound yet simple ritual leads to no magic fixing of horrors or broken hearts; and there is no heroic gesture required. Rabbi Brous urges us to simply see one another in our full humanity and whenever possible, show up, to "err on the side of presence."[18]

Rabbi Brous makes two additional, special points that are particularly meaningful for our modern, divided times. Firstly, that this grace of being seen was extended to the ostracized and excommunicated, too. While they were prohibited from most of the rest of society's rituals and spaces, they were invited to this one. The ancient rabbis considered no one disposable, even those who had seriously harmed their community.

Secondly, we humans lean toward the known. We find comfort, order, meaning and purpose, and pride in our tribes. Especially during times of crisis and trauma. But our instinct to lean toward our tribe can be dangerous; the more we turn that way, the more we might dismiss or feel hostility toward those outside it. Rabbi Brous writes, "One of the great casualties of tribalism is curiosity."[19] And when curiosity wanes, imagination, understanding, and empathy wane along with it.

I'm intrigued by what might be a modern form, maybe a more secular form, of coming together in community to ask life's biggest questions. To mourn the passing of life, celebrate life passages, ponder, help, volunteer, and do service together.

Imagine this is you. You are searching for community, comradery, sharing, witnessing, and accompaniment. Imagine you are the convener, and you're adding a leaf to your kitchen table. Think beyond who the usual suspects might be, to expand—by a leaf or two—who are your people. If we stick to the usual inhabitants of our kitchen tables, we can tend toward echo chambers and tribalism. The goal is to thoughtfully and intentionally add people from outside the usuals, so as to keep the sparks of curiosity, imagination, learning, and empathy kindling.

Invitation, seeing and accompanying, listening, being present. These simple yet deeply human actions are behaviors we all can do. In faith communities, the church or temple provides the home for us to do them. I think we can invite, listen, witness, and accompany in secular spaces, too.

. . .

FINDING NEW WAYS to be in community is not always easy, but it's important to be open to the chance everyday interactions, to be present, to try to show up for each other, to value the cultural aspects of charitable work, and to dig for and appreciate the connections between philanthropic practice and our cultures and heritages. And from here, it's a small step to turn that community into a force for good. Mutual aid groups and giving circles add intentionality to these spaces through action.

Mutual aid groups are neighbors helping neighbors. They're another way to form community, and we've always come together in this way. Emphasizing a focus on "solidarity, not charity," mutual aid centers cooperation because, as Mariame Kaba, an educator, activist, and organizer writes, "We recognize that our well-being, health, and dignity are all bound up in each other."[20] Mutual aid groups tend to be quick, responsive, and flexible, finding and providing what people need rather than giving what donors want to give. It is estimated that tens of thousands of mutual aid groups sprang up in the early days of COVID.[21] From organizing local childcare, to legal aid, to putting together food baskets, to sewing squads, neighbors and strangers gave money, volunteered time, donated skills, and joined together in solidarity to support one another. When anti-Asian hate spiked in New York City, mutual aid groups sprang up to provide free escort for Asian Americans doing errands around the city.

There is a rich history of mutual aid groups in America, especially among people of color, queer, and immigrant communities. The Free African Society was started in 1787 in Philadelphia by two ministers, Richard Allen and Absalom Jones. It was one of the first Black mutual aid societies in America, and it organized its members to offer relief to the sick, shelter orphans, and transport and bury the dead. Black mutual aid societies grew rapidly in the early 1800s. By 1830, there were one hundred mutual aid societies in Philadelphia, thirty in Baltimore, and many more up and down the country from Boston to New Orleans.

David Ruggles, a conductor on the Underground Railroad, organized the New York Committee of Vigilance in 1835. He called it "practical abolition" to confront slave catchers, advocate for Black people in court, and to generally provide assistance, succor, relief, advice, education, food, and housing for Black people, including, famously, Frederick Douglass. Vigilance committees sprang up in cities like Cleveland, Albany, Detroit, and Philadelphia, funded primarily by Black women who ran bake sales, sold crafts, and pooled money. By the turn of the century, 15 percent of Black men and 52 percent of Black women in New York City belonged to a mutual aid society.

In the 1900s, immigrant groups across the country found protection, power, and solidarity by sticking together. They helped each other fight racism and nativism, find shelter, jobs, legal defense, personal loans, medical care, insurance, English-language classes, and even family and other connections. They also held social events to foster the community. Some of these included the Chinese Consolidated Benevolent Society in San Francisco, Landsmanshaftn for Jewish immigrants in New York City, and Sociedades Mutualistas for Mexican immigrants to the Southwest.

Famously, the Black Panthers started the Free Breakfast for Children Program in Oakland, California, in 1969. They created dozens of "survival" programs like free ambulance services, rides for elderly people to do errands, and community health clinics. The free breakfast program—cooking and serving breakfasts for local children in Oakland because of the overwhelming evidence that a healthy breakfast is beneficial for health and learning—is one of the most famous examples of mutual aid in modern times. The Black Panthers solicited donations from local restaurants and neighbors, and the program quickly expanded to forty-five cities around the country, feeding fifty thousand kids. The FBI shut it down by raiding cafeterias and, in one notorious incident, peeing on food to destroy it, but soon afterward started a federal free breakfast program. The Black Panthers Free Breakfast for Children Program remains the gold standard example of grassroots community organizing.

In New York City's East Harlem and Lower East Side neighborhoods, the Young Lords, a group of young Puerto Rican activists, organized a Garbage Offensive in 1969. They'd been spearheading garbage cleanups every Sunday because the sanitation department neglected their neighborhoods to such a degree that they were overflowing with trash. Neighbors came out to help. One day, angry that the city wouldn't provide more brooms, they pushed the garbage into the middle of the street and set it ablaze. That got some attention from the media, and the city was forced to clean it up. The Young Lords' other mutual aid efforts included free daycare and breakfast programs, door-to-door TB testing, and in one case, taking over a mobile-TB X-ray truck that was skipping their neighborhoods.

In the 1980s and 1990s, as more and more gay men began dying of AIDS, often stigmatized and alone, Tim Burak, a volunteer at a Seattle health clinic, proposed a "buddy network" where people could volunteer to help grocery-shop, do chores, drive, and provide home companionship for ill people. This turned into the Chicken Soup Brigade, an all-volunteer group that grew to support over 450 men.

I travel to New Mexico often because my parents live there. During COVID lockdowns, dozens of mutual aid efforts emerged, including one that characterized itself as "Just enough to get people through—not a gallon of bleach, but a 4-ounce mason jar of it, half a dozen diapers, a few cups of beans, a bag of potatoes, some vegetables, a pound of hamburger meat. Almost every day, Albuquerque Mutual Aid volunteers sanitize and pack items, then load them into cars . . . The goal: fast, responsive care, particularly for those who might fall through the cracks."[22] That goal could describe the thousands of mutual aid groups that spring into action during crises around the country and that provide ongoing critical charitable services in communities.

Mutual aid groups often bring all the *T*'s into their work: time, talent, treasure, testimony, and ties. My wonderful agent, Maggie, is in one in her neighborhood near Boston. What might it look like to step into this rich history of mutual aid societies, in your building, block, or neighborhood? We've been practicing generosity in all sorts of ways, always. I hope learning about how others are doing it sparks some ideas in you.

GIVING CIRCLES, like religious communities and mutual aid groups, not only allow us to come together to do good, but also act as a form of support in tough times, strengthening our ties to our community and to each other. During the height of the COVID pandemic, many of us experienced loneliness of a whole other tenor and magnitude. There was also a surge of anti-Asian hate crimes in New York City. One of my Asian Women Giving Circle (AWGC) sisters was spat on, another was pushed onto a sidewalk, I was shoulder-shoved at a Trader Joe's. We all experienced the stares, the "get out" and "go home" looks and words, the "you don't belong here" sentiments. Our friend, renowned activist and photographer Corky Lee, had died of COVID. It was a dark time for many of us.

When the Atlanta spa shootings happened on March 16, 2021, the AWGC became something more for many of us. The police captain in Atlanta described the killer as having had "a really bad day." The entitlement was breathtaking. So was the patriarchal attempt to minimize the brutal murders. The murders of Asian American women spa workers was the perfect storm, the toxic collision of racism, misogyny, hate toward immigrants, social class, economic decisions, the sexual fetishizing of Asian women—all of it. We sisters of the AWGC, we got it.

One of my AWGC sisters, Lu, remembered that time with me recently. She said, "I don't know where I'd be if I didn't have the giving circle. We could share honestly how afraid we were. How sad we were, especially amid the aftermath of the murder of George Floyd and the reckoning of race, class, ethnicity. For me as an Asian, I had to step back and decenter myself. Others were more in need and were being marginalized like crazy. Then anti-Asian hate started happening more. In some progressive spaces, it can feel weird to center myself. The only place that felt right and welcoming, a first step to voice my own experience, was the Asian Women Giving Circle. I cried on our Zoom call. I rarely cry. It started a thawing, a softening, the beginning of not being so afraid."

The giving circle has become a place where Lu and all of us can practice being more free, more authentic, because as she said, "You all were modeling what it means to be in community, to show you're in pain. I needed to see my own people do that, even cry. Especially older yous. There's this notion of permission. I needed to see other members do it. I saw you talk about it and cry. I saw Melinda scream about it. I saw Nam with tears in her eyes. The social cues we seek out, as younger Asian people; we seek permission to do certain things. We assume you can't do things, like in our households, that's how we were raised. Oh, you can cry about this? We can show emotions. We can say the Atlanta shootings were wrong, racialized, gendered, xenophobic. All the intersections. Now I know how my identity feeds into my work, my purpose in philanthropy, my social justice work. Just by seeing you do it, I feel like I can do that, too. Let me try that here where it's safe. Practice. Now I can try at work, with my friends."

The beating heart of the Asian Women Giving Circle is the relationships we are building with one another. The beating heart of community activism is the relationships between and among the community members who are working together to improve their neighborhoods. The beating heart of doing philanthropy well is tending to the community and the relationships therein. Community can become giving circles, and giving circles can become community. Both have to do with building belonging.

FRANK LIU is a slim, stylish, bighearted, soft-spoken man who lives in Chelsea, Manhattan. He's had a long career in advertising, branding, and marketing and launched his own consulting firm, Brand Justice, in 2021. Frank had been part of a group of gay men who met monthly for nice dinners out. He'd also been coming regularly to Asian Women Giving Circle events and was a regular donor. Partly inspired by the AWGC, he had this idea to ask the dinner guys if they'd like to add a charitable component to their monthly get-togethers. The guys agreed and The Dinner Guys was born. We proudly consider them our brother circle. Instead of going out to a fancy restaurant, they began to take turns hosting potlucks or going on picnics, and they decided to put the extra cash into a giving circle pot. Around the same time, one of the Guys became aware of SAGE, a nonprofit organization in New York City that provides community and services for older gay men, many of whom are lonely. At the time of The Dinner Guys' founding, SAGE had two Asian American people participating in its programs. After The Dinner Guys started sending them donations ranging from $5,000 to $10,000 per year, totaling $42,000 over the years, SAGE was able to add outreach into Asian communities as part of their regular programming. Immediately, older gay Asian American men started participating in the welcoming SAGE community. And this small but momentous change was brought about because of one giving circle of connected citizens who knew their community's needs and took action to bring about change for the better.

Frank and The Dinner Guys keep it super simple. They're not interested in recruiting new members or expanding the circle. They give away what they raise themselves. They keep it local and intimate. Yet they've made profound change in the LGBTQ+ community in New York City.

Through many years of friendship, The Dinner Guys were a solid crew of friends, united by their love of good food and their shared identity as gay New Yorkers. They had the inspiration to share the love by expanding their circle outward to elder gay men who sought belonging and community, too. They turned the belonging they'd built with each other and spread it like magic dust to build belonging among a larger community of gay men in New York City. The Dinner Guys added purpose, doing good together, and money to the thing they'd been doing for many years. And they've built belonging within their group and within their larger community.

Building belonging can be like that; it's contagious, magical, and feels great. Underneath the endeavor is love of humanity. But to get there, to have the idea and desire to build belonging in the first place, The Dinner Guys had to talk about what mattered most to them. And that means talking about values.

5

The Values We Share

What turns a group of friends, neighbors, or colleagues into a giving circle? There are two key factors: shared values and money. They're intimately related because every time we spend money, it's an expression of our values.

And it's the shared-values bit that sets giving circles apart from much of Big Phil philanthropy. Before we can get to the Big We, we've got to talk about the Big "Why:" Why do we care, what is the "why" of our work, or as an old colleague used to say, "What's the point of us?"

Values are the beliefs and attitudes that guide our actions. Each and every one of us has core values that represent what we care about and that guide our behaviors. It is foundationally important to think about our values when we're considering embarking on a thoughtful philanthropy practice. Values are important touchstones that can help us navigate the choices and decisions we'll face and inform the way we want to show up in the world.

The practice of philanthropy has become awfully transactive—a person with resources donates money to a cause or organization, and the relationship, if there is one, is largely around the money. Little is learned on either side of the transaction. No one knows more about the other person's wants, needs, wishes, fears, or dreams. Transactions are a necessary component, but in order to achieve authentic community building and lasting social change, transactions alone are inadequate.

Just like the novels are missing from the spreadsheets of technocratic, strategic philanthropy, human stories, values, compassion, love, sadness, and joy are missing from giving that is solely transactional. The thing we are chasing, after all, is freedom, more opportunity for all, equal access to the promise of this country's founding principles. In other words, what we are seeking is transformation, not a series of transactions.

Kate Rigg, a.k.a. Lady K-Sian (who also performs with Lyris Hung as the divine duo Slanty Eyed Mama), is a Juilliard-trained musician, spoken word artist, actor, comedian, writer, and performance queen. She is profane and profound and we love her. She has received multiple grants from the AWGC for works like the rock opera *Americasiana* and *The Urban Tao*, which look at the American dream through Asian American eyes. Kate told us that receiving a grant from the AWGC felt like having a big bunch of noisy aunties cheering on the sidelines. It's honestly the best thing I've heard, ever, about us as grantmakers.

Sure, there is money involved, and financial transactions have taken place. We've paid Kate for emceeing and performing at our events, and Kate has received multiple grants from the AWGC. But our relationship with, and support for, her goes far beyond that. We've been audience members for her performances all over New York City. We see each other at other cultural happenings. We've referred and nominated Kate for multiple other awards and stages. I wish we had more money to give Kate and other genius artist activists like her. We can give more than money, though—all of our Five T's of time, talent, treasure, testimony, and ties to help Kate and us move our values in the world, with joy and in community.

How did we find our collective "why?" In the case of the Asian Women Giving Circle, this looked like two or three group conversations. And we revisit our group's "why" about once a year.

For the AWGC, between meetings number one and two, I had an aha moment in the shower. Most of us in that first group of ten women were former, current, or wanna-be artists. Lisa looks like a librarian but had a side gig as a DJ. BJ was a lawyer by day and music producer by night. Shinhee had been an avid painter. We have several writers in the group. I've aspired to be a sculptor and potter and, today, am an avid creator of misshapen knitted things. We all believed in the power of working together for equitable social change. We knew in our bones that culture change is a necessary precondition for social change. So here was the germ of our collective "why." We would raise and give away money in support of Asian American women and gender-expansive folks who were using the tools of arts and culture to move equitable social change in our New York City communities.

In order to get to that aha moment in the shower, I had to be curious about these women, now giving circle sisters. We had to spend time getting to know one another. We had to talk about our cultural and familial money stories, like what did we learn about spending, saving, generosity, sharing, and scarcity growing up? From whom did we learn these things? On whose shoulders do we stand to do this work, and what kind of ancestor do I want to be for the future generations about whom I can only dream? We talked about work, family, and extracurricular activities, like where we volunteer and where we give our time and discretionary dollars. Where do we spend our Five T's? What moves you, what keeps you up at night? What are the burning issues facing our Asian American New York City communities right now, and how might a group of well-meaning, well-connected women help?

Giving circles thrive when we can approach the nuts and bolts of giving with a clear sense of the group's shared "why." What is the change the group is trying to make in the world (be it their neighborhood, block, city, or beyond)? What would they love to see happen in their neighborhood? Which means that before anyone cuts a check, it's important to have some thoughtful conversations. It is powerful to sit in an intimate space and unearth shared dreams, visions, fears, and worries. Lightly facilitated conversations like these encourage bonding and the building of relationships that go deeper than the more superficial layers one might reach during a dinner or cocktail party.

AS YOU MAY remember from part 1, large swaths of philanthropy prioritize metrics over values. Some philanthropy advisors and organizations hold it as a value to be values-agnostic, which I find very counterintuitive. How can you move money into the world without having some idea of why or what for?

In a direct response to this values-neutral norm in our sector, my truly beloved Radiant Strategies team, Letarik Amare and Isis Krause, and I, along with Ayushi Vig, built a 100 percent unabashedly values-centric philanthropy curriculum in 2020 called Freedom School for Philanthropy. It was funded, in part, by the W. K. Kellogg Foundation, the Bill & Melinda Gates Foundation, Fidelity Charitable, and the Raikes Foundation.

The curriculum is built for wealthy donors who aim to center equity in their philanthropic practice. We have two primary goals: to move more resources, faster, to leaders and organizations working toward equitable social change; and to exercise the organizing and influencing muscle in those folks who are interested.

Because I was writing it at the same time as this book, it's maybe not a surprise that the curriculum follows a Me to We to Big We arc. It starts with the personal, familial, cultural, then moves to workplaces and other groups, then finally, to our larger communities, cities, society, our democracy. Values are in the first section (the Me section), and we state up top, "Values are everything, especially in philanthropy."

Rather than start with the donor (a radical idea in philanthropy), we started with the people on the ground doing the work. The first thing we did to build Freedom School for Philanthropy was interview a dozen movement leaders and executive directors of nonprofits. We asked them to describe their relationships with individual donors, specifically the attributes of those relationships that were mutually beneficial, rewarding, even transformational. Then we asked them to describe those relationships with donors that were, in a word, shitty. By *shitty* I mean relationships in which they may have felt used, or extracted from, or in which the relationships were largely transactional, or in which they felt less than human, like a dog in a dog-and-pony show, or a cog in a machine of the donor's creation. We built Freedom School for Philanthropy largely informed by the wishes and guidance of the organizational and movement leaders we interviewed.

Building this curriculum is our effort to put values front and center, where they belong, particularly in philanthropic settings and practices. In a group, talking about, saying out loud, and discussing our values helps others understand our goals and motivations. Especially when there is disagreement, it is really important to have some grounding in your personal values and the group's shared values.

The premise and inspiration of Freedom School for Philanthropy is that our fates are linked, or as civil rights icon Fannie Lou Hamer famously said, "Nobody's free until everybody's free." But we live in a time where the idea of freedom is deeply contested in America. Is freedom something that is won in free markets or in democratic forums? Is it zero sum or can it be something that we all have equal access to? The "tragedy of the commons" describes what happens when individualistic freedom runs its inexorable course. Imagine a beautiful, green pasture open to all. If you're a cattle farmer who wants to maximize your profit, you have an incentive to own as many heads of cattle as you can and for your cattle to eat as much grass as possible on that shared pasture. But if all the other farmers do the same thing, the field will soon be overgrazed and ruined. The inherent logic of the commons leads relentlessly and remorselessly to a ruined pasture, which is the tragedy of this commons. Each farmer, being a rational actor, is locked into a system that compels him to add animal after animal without limit, in a world that is inherently limited. When people take more than they need, resources held in common are at risk.

We can see examples all around us of individualistic freedom run amok—the alarming draining of aquifers that provide groundwater for all, industries that act like individuals polluting the air and causing asthma rates to rise, easy access to weapons of war that kill innocent people in mass shootings.

We also accept limitations on our individual freedoms to benefit the larger good, the commons. Though we may love to drive fast, we accept that speed limits on highways (and stop signs at busy intersections) are good for public safety. Though we love letting our dogs run free, we accept leash laws in parks during busy hours. Most Americans think it's a good idea for children to get vaccinated against measles, diphtheria, tetanus, and chicken pox before they attend schools, for public health reasons.

What happens if we reimagine the commons as this beautiful, almost sacred thing that we all share and are responsible for—the air, the oceans, our land, a tiny little community garden?

What happens if we reimagine ourselves within the commons, metaphorically and literally? Indigenous folks talk about being custodians of the land. What might we be willing to give up in order for all of us to be free?

My college buddy David Hughes is a born-and-bred Californian. He loves to surf and skinny-dip. He's been an ecologist, climate activist, advocate against cars and airplanes, walker, biker, kayaker, saver, recycler, and re-user since high school—rare in the mid-1980s. Once, so irate that a car had blocked the pedestrian walkway, he walked himself and his bike over the hood, to the astonishment of the flabbergasted driver. We occasionally fear for David's life.

David is now an anthropology professor at Rutgers University and remains a dear friend. He wrote a book in 2021, *Who Owns the Wind: Climate Crisis and the Hope of Renewable Energy.* David makes the argument, through the stories and lives of real people who live in the Spanish town where he did much of his research, that the energy revolution we need will come about only if we make it fair. Renewable energies like wind and solar are the way forward to stabilize our climate. We've got to figure out a way for wind, solar, and other renewables to be equated with fairness for all, rather than private gain for few. Wind ought to be considered a common resource, something that tangibly benefits the communities where turbines are located. He suggests that even if the land underneath the wind is privately owned, the kinetic energy made by the wind ought to be owned and shared by the people in the community, not just the landowner who puts up the turbine. His book is a paean to seize a democratic path toward plentiful renewable energy that is fossil fuel–free and community owned.

Individualistic, heroic, technocratic, richest-guy-wins thinking and acting is ruining our planet. Can we subvert these attributes and reimagine our commons to lead to something greener and fairer?

Freedom School for Philanthropy asks philanthropists to think more about the commons in a way that decenters themselves, prioritizes values, and centers community—a people-powered philanthropy rather than a billionaire-powered one. I sometimes think of it as changing the subject. Let's change the subject of the philanthropic story away from the donor (the Me) and toward the community (the We).

We need another frame. We need to think more like a We than a Me. Giving circles are a natural vehicle to get us there.

THERE'S AN ART, and an arc, to turning a group of friends, neighbors, or colleagues into a giving circle, and the arc goes from Me to We to Big We.

In order to authentically engage with others around social change, we've got to start with ourselves, the Me. But the key is to not stop there, we've got to keep on going. Social change is deep, meaningful, long-haul work, and to build the trust and relationships that are needed to sustain it, we've got to know our own "why." Why the heck do I care? Who do I come from, who are my people? What are my heartaches? What are my most cherished values that will guide me when things get tough, because shared values become our most constant, inspirational north stars.

To dive deeper into your own "why," ask yourself, What is my family's money story? How did money, generosity, and scarcity flow in my family? Who in my family tree were the changemakers, imagination-people dreamers, activists, even freedom fighters like my grandfather? Who in my family tree were the traditionalists, culture-bearers, maybe even culture-overbearers? What are my most cherished values, and how do these values get translated into actions in the world? How do my most cherished values get translated into my vision for what I want the world to be for my children and grandchildren? All this goes into the "Me." Ideally, each of us who is engaged in making our communities better is able to articulate our own reasons why we're in this work. It's important that we do this lifelong exercise so we can find partners and like-minded travelers to join together on this journey toward the We.

Many of us are part of several We groups. You might be in a book, parenting, hiking, running, alumnae, or collegial work group; faith community; adult sports team, professional society, or a fraternal/sororal organization. For me, my We groups are my family, the Asian Women Giving Circle, my Radiant Strategies teammates, the growing community of donors who are part of the Freedom School for Philanthropy community, my block association (go SoPo!), occasionally a former stitch-n-bitch group, and sometimes my college buddy group. Any of these groups can morph into a giving circle by adding conversations around shared purpose and values and money. To establish the shared values in a group that is trying to move from community to collective action, the group might talk about what priorities and concerns members share. Or some actions that they might like to do together, like volunteer at a nonprofit, write postcards for issues or candidates, attend a book talk on an issue they care about, or even go to a march or rally. It's always fruitful to talk about one another's core values and where they came from, then as a group identify shared values and shared family experiences.

I remember at the first gathering of the brand-new Donors of Color Network at Tamaya in New Mexico, I saw an almost-sixty-year-old Korean American woman and a forty-year-old Panamanian American woman hugging and crying at the snack table as they shared familial stories of parents who sacrificed everything to move their families to the United States, the shared preeminently important value of education in their families, and their hopes and struggles around keeping some of those family lessons and values alive and thriving in their teenage and young adult children. From radically different backgrounds and life experiences, these two women had found belonging with each other, and it was beautiful.

It was our hope then, as we were building the Donors of Color Network, that it would be connections like these that would undergird the solidarity and allyship that would be necessary if we were ever to succeed in building a cross-race network of people who do good, hard work together. Our capacity as individuals across wildly different life experiences, backgrounds, faiths, cultures, and traditions to find common ground and linkages is the starting point, the foundation, upon which we can live into the promise of building a pluralistic democracy on this land. Listening, sharing, witnessing, and accompaniment were important skills.

For some folks, talking with others about family, money, and shared values might feel too intimate, or rather big and scary. But it has been my experience that, overwhelmingly, it's worth it to push through the discomfort, gently and together. In the end, most people are thrilled to have an opportunity to talk about deeply held values, beliefs, hopes, and dreams—and their familial and cultural underpinnings. Each person will appreciate knowing the others more deeply and personally. People will leave these get-togethers feeling as if their souls, hearts, and brains have been fed.

For shorthand, I sometimes keep this simple phrase in mind—*from Me to We*. It will become a reminder that connecting each person's individual story to the group's story is a way to continuously knit people together. The threads of those connections will help any group weather disagreements that come up and will increase each person's connection to the larger purpose and work in the community.

FOR ALL OUR community-minded DNA and spirit, giving circles are still part of the philanthropy ecosystem in the United States. And certainly, a group of individuals can be just as paternalistic and overbearing as any one individual donor can be. If you put a bunch of jerks into a group together, they don't magically become better humans just because they're in a group. Reifying things like paternalism and top-down power dynamics cannot be the goal. As a circle gets started, its members might well be a little bit like that out-of-touch billionaire. Circle members will investigate their own and the group's values, and they will probably learn a lot about a community issue they don't know much about in order to move the group's values and resources into the world. There will be mistakes made, learning curves to navigate, and the inherent power dynamic that exists in philanthropy. These are fundamental tensions in philanthropy, and I navigate them daily, not always well.

One big, central, inherent tension that most if not all social changemakers feel—at least the ones who are not oblivious or nihilists or torch throwers—is this: we work within a thing that we are simultaneously trying to change. I work within the philanthropic sector at the same time I am trying to nudge it to change. I work with wealthy individual donors at the same time that I think the wealth gap and racial wealth gap are unsustainable, undemocratic, and shameful. I can vote and advocate for higher taxes on the very wealthy at the same time that I work with some very wealthy people and foundations to move more of their resources to support human dignity, flourishing, freedom, equity, and joy.

This tension in philanthropy, between donor intent (even groups of donors) and community needs, is a conundrum because what really matters is the social good in the world, but in order to move private resources toward that social good, we must (at least for now) necessarily factor in donor wishes, intent, and values.

Because so much of the wealth in the United States is concentrated in the hands of the very richest among us, philanthropy bends its heads their way, like flowers to the sun. And because the accumulation of wealth in the United States is racialized and gendered, philanthropy tends to bend toward the white and male. The wishes, intent, values, and vision of the donor class carry outsize import in our field and sector.

Collectives and giving circles ameliorate that tension somewhat because we are inherently a more democratic form. We give in groups, which means there is usually some sort of group decision-making, and this tends to rule out monarchs, dictators, and autocrats. Often, giving circles are closer to the communities into which we send money. In the case of the AWGC, the lines are blurry between the folks we fund and the folks we are. For instance, at least one of us usually has to recuse herself from our annual funding discussions because we're on the board of an applying organization or run one or used to run one or it's our sister-in-law's.

PHILANTHROPY IS AN expression of culture. The way we practice philanthropy has become separated from our roots. We've strayed too far toward the transactive nature of an exchange, and away from the possible transformations with and in our communities. Historically, the practice of philanthropy has always been intrinsically connected to cultural practices of mutuality, care, community, generosity, humility, and belonging, and when aunties and grandmothers are involved, probably a fair bit of cheekiness too.

Andine is one of my Asian Women Giving Circle sisters. Her grandmother and mom have always participated in Indonesian *arisan*. In an *arisan*, people put money into the *arisan* pot, then they put names into a box, and whoever's name is drawn takes the pot. Andine's grandmother had eleven siblings, and after the war of independence in 1945, each sibling emerged in dramatically different economic situations. They started a sibling *arisan* as a way to help each other out that didn't feel like a handout, because each sibling put something in. Her grandmother had more, so she would often put extra money into the *arisan*. Sometimes she would put another sibling's name into the box, not hers. No one knows exactly what the others are contributing. It's a way to be generous without incurring any social obligation or guilt.

Andine's grandmother was often in multiple *arisans* at the same time. One time, she came home all giggly and tickled because unbeknownst to a friend who'd suffered a financial loss recently, all the other *arisan* ladies had put that member's name into the box. So the friend in need got that *arisan*. She was able to get help without the potential embarrassment of having to ask for it. Independence and self-sufficiency are valued, so culturally, it can be hard to ask for help. Andine says, "It's engineered in all these cheeky ways—my grandmother will sometimes put three of her siblings into the box so the probability goes up that one of them might get chosen. The intentionality is sweet."

There are so many beautiful and moving values in Andine's grandmother's *arisan*. Among them, generosity, humility, helping each other with respect, mutuality, and care. Community. Connecting to roots. Belonging. Cheekiness. You can feel the love flowing all throughout, and the profound consideration for one another's dignity. Plus I love the playfulness, which helps keep practices like this going for years.

THE CURRENT TREND of strategic philanthropy, tech-bro philanthropy, logic models, KPIs (key performance indicators), impact-driven giving, "show me the proof and I'll show you the money," giving divorced from values, giving divorced from culture, us-versus-them giving—it is all this that is ahistoric and anomalous. Humans have always helped humans. *Gehs, arisans, tandas,* and *sou sous* exist in almost every culture. In every major religious tradition, there is something like tithing or *zakat* or *tzedakah* or *dāna*.

Faith practices and philanthropy have always been deeply intertwined, and because of that, ideas around morality naturally arise. Conversations having to do with values may be off-putting or scary because we don't want to come across as preachy or sanctimonious. Some of us are suspicious of religion and morality, or even disparage people of faith. And some of us shun people who fall outside our tribe, our morality, and our religion. But I think we need to be able to face our outrage, even our moral indignation, when the circumstances warrant it. In my college days, we activated for Princeton University to disinvest from South Africa's apartheid regime. Using our power as consumers to boycott and the power of our voice to protest are peaceful, honorable ways to disagree with government actions. As citizens who care, we come face-to-face with these "bigger We" moments, and it is only by standing in our values that we can navigate them.

I also think that there is much around which we Americans can agree. We can all espouse humanistic values and act in solidarity when we see harm. I think we all want our children to be able to live up to their full potential. We can all think and talk about what is a social contract and what is my role in a social contract with my fellow citizens. Most of us can agree that we have an individual responsibility to our families, neighbors, workplaces, groups, cities. Most of us think more of us should vote. Most of us pay taxes, albeit with varying degrees of fervor. Most of us aspire to be good neighbors, good colleagues, good parents, good aunties and uncles, and good friends.

As a sector, we've tried separating values and giving, but we can't, and we shouldn't. Values and giving have always been intertwined, and giving circles are one way to put that critical element back into our giving practice.

FARHAD EBRAHIMI is a dad, a partner, and a deeply principled person who is unafraid of being a values-forward, occasionally morally indignant philanthropist. He wrestles with this conundrum of trying to change a thing while living in it in his philanthropic practice. Farhad inherited what he calls an obscene amount of money from his father before he was twenty-one. His father is one of the cofounders of Quark, which was a pioneer in word processing and then graphic design. Farhad's familial backgrounds are Iranian, Irish, and Cuban. Both his mom and dad experienced revolutions in their home countries and, subsequently, lived through escaping and becoming refugees. Farhad's personal and political journey included punk rock, and in that scene, he says, "We accept you for the misfit you are."

When his father gave him and his sister a big chunk of cash, Farhad kind of freaked out. He thought it was insane that his father had so much money to begin with, and that he'd give so much to him and his sister when they were so young. Over the next few years, Farhad embarked on a crash course in philanthropy, learning from mentors and Resource Generation, a network of wealthy young people under the age of thirty-five. He created the Chorus Foundation as a "spend down" foundation, meaning that from its outset, it would spend down its assets over ten years. Chorus closed in 2023 after having given out $60 to $65 million over its lifetime.

Farhad is something of a philanthropy philosopher. He calls philanthropy a transitional form, meaning it's a necessary-evil-type-step toward a future when there isn't such wealth disparity to begin with. He believes that there shouldn't be such a concentration of wealth in the hands of such a very few. Chorus decided to spend down in ten years in order to return wealth to communities from whom it had been taken. And as we've seen from the data on wealth disparities, assets build upon assets, so returning some helps communities build up again.

Most giving circles are probably not thinking about spending down or distributing $60 million over ten years. But maybe you will find some inspiration in Farhad, who thinks about returning wealth to communities from which it's been extracted. In one community that Chorus invested in, Kentuckians for the

Commonwealth, wealth was literally stripped from coal mines and those who worked in them, with very little of that wealth staying in the communities (or with the workers and their families) most affected. So being a values-centered philanthropist and a generally principled, smart guy, Farhad steered his foundation toward repatriating some of that wealth back into the communities from which it had been taken. Chorus has taken a similar values-grounded, community-centered approach in Alaska, Richmond, CA, and Buffalo, NY.

I admire Farhad's principled stance and his ability to face his vision for a bigger We than his own family's wealth. Farhad is unafraid to be morally indignant about the very fact that such wealth disparities exist, even as he and his family benefit from it. Giving circles can also take principled positions in the face of injustices happening in their communities. There might very well be a giving circle in Kentucky that is raising money collectively to put back into communities from whom wealth, in the form of ore and coal, has been stripped. In fact, on the Philanthropy Together website, there are over twenty giving circles in Kentucky, including in the counties of Jessamine, Shelby, Elizabeth, Oldham, Henry, Owensboro, and Cookeville, and several in the cities of Louisville and Lexington, and a few statewide and regionals to boot. There's a States Project giving circle in Kentucky, which is focused on building power in state legislatures. There are men's, women's, faith-inspired, and youth/teen circles, too. I'd love to know if there has been any cross-pollination between Farhad's work and the local giving circles, but either way, I'm energized to know that so many Kentuckians are coming together to help one another. We need these grassroots efforts along with the millionaires, and imagine the power that could be unleashed if there was collaboration between them!

. . .

FOR THE ASIAN WOMEN GIVING CIRCLE, one of our animating values is mutual care, belonging, and supporting our sisterhood. We start every meeting with a personal check-in. Sometimes, when there's a lot going on, the whole meeting might be the personal check-in. While that can be frustrating for those of us who love an agenda, over time, it's so worth it to prioritize the relationships. It is these personal connections that will help the group weather disagreements and rough patches. This kind of deep engagement is an end in itself—a balm to our feelings of loneliness and atomization—but also a crucial first step to the work we hope to do together. When it comes to the problems we aim to address, conversation and connection aren't enough alone, but they are a critical starting point.

These conversations are not always easy, however. Conflict is a natural part of being in community. And sometimes people part ways because of a misalignment around values.

Affirmative action is an important and divisive topic, especially among Asian Americans. The Supreme Court gutted affirmative action in the summer of 2023, ruling that admissions at Harvard and the University of North Carolina (therefore all universities) must be colorblind. The plaintiffs at Harvard included a group of Asian American students who claimed that affirmative action hurt their chances to get into Ivy League schools. In New York City, the elite public high schools are known as "specialized" high schools. They're very hard to get into, and the most prestigious among them have disproportionally high percentages of Asian kids. When then Mayor Bill de Blasio proposed doing away with the standardized test that determines admission in 2019, a group of Asian parents protested.[1] Those of us who support affirmative action have been called "race traitors" by some of our Asian American brothers, sisters, and cousins.

The Asian Women Giving Circle lost a member because we disagreed about affirmative action. Minh is Vietnamese Chinese and had elementary-aged kids at the time. She thought that affirmative action would hurt her kids' chances of getting into New York City's best public high schools and, later, into the most selective colleges. We'd had some conversations about the topic in general during meetings, and some of us had done some activism in support of affirmative action. There was no official group position or stance, but individually, most of us were and are in support of efforts to address systemic inequalities and are in favor of cross-race solidarity efforts, with affirmative action being one.

"Even Overs" are a useful tool when one must make a choice between two good things. To use a food analogy, for me, French fries *even over* potato chips. Or devils' food chocolate cake *even over* a brownie. For me, the value at work here is We *even over* Me.

I choose cross-race solidarity especially when it helps a group that has been unfairly treated historically and systemically, *even over* Asian Americans in this case. Moreover, I know that pitting one group against another is a well-worn and effective strategy that works against building cross-race solidarity and freedom for all.

Minh had eyes mostly on her own family and children. She saw affirmative action as a threat to their potential success. She took the group's temperature and decided to leave. It wasn't dramatic; there was no fight. We'd had civil and serious conversations about affirmative action, and its impacts on various groups of Asian Americans, and other groups, in New York City and nationally. Minh decided it didn't make sense for her to continue to be part of those conversations when her values differed from ours, though she still stays in touch with the circle and various of our members.

Although I was sorry to see Minh go, I was proud of all of us for having civil discussions and abiding by what was most important to us.

How we are with one another is how we build the world we want to live in.

THERE IS ONE last value I believe should undergird all philanthropic activity, and that is humility. We social-change types can get sanctimonious, holier-than-thou, and arrogant. We can demand and expect purity, allegiance, and absolutism. We can verge on being one-note, droning evangelists for our cause.

We live in an era full of aggrieved people. The insurrectionists who stormed the Capitol on January 6, 2021, were a dangerous, frenzied mob. As Frank Bruni wrote in an op-ed recently, "But above all, they were unhumble. They decided that they held the truth, no matter all the evidence to the contrary."[2]

Bruni teaches at Duke University and says of his role, "I'm standing before them [my students] not as an ambassador of certainty or a font of unassailable verities but as an emissary of doubt. I want to give them intelligent questions, not final answers. I want to teach them how much they have to learn—and how much they will always have to learn."[3] Uplift curiosity, lifelong learning, imagination, making mistakes, getting up and trying again. Humility and the mindset of being a lifelong learner are bulwarks against conceit and sanctimony. Find the gray areas, revel in the grays in fact, and keep on learning.

I remember in social work grad school, one of my professors noted that a marker of mental health is the ability to hold ambiguity. In other words, a marker of mental wellness is the ability to see and appreciate life's many grays and not devolve to black-and-white, or binary, thinking. Rarely is there one right answer. Often, there are many good answers, many good actions, or many good-enough responses.

Aligning on shared values is a critical first step to transform a group of friends, neighbors, or colleagues into a giving circle. And it will prepare everyone for the more difficult, but equally necessary, step two: money.

6

Let's Talk About Money

Money is a human invention. Humans created currency to help people trade goods and services. We invented banks so that travelers wouldn't have to lug around heavy forms of currency that might not even be recognized in a neighboring region. We invented tax codes so that governments could pay for public goods and services and go to war. Philanthropy exists as a profession—along with wealth advisory, accounting, trust and estate law—to deal with, in some ways, an excess of money.

How we spend our money says something about what we think is important and what our values are. The Jesuits put it best in a letter exhorting the U.S. Congress to care for our nation's poor: "Budgets are moral documents. They reveal priorities and values, and as a society, they are the primary way we care for one another, especially the vulnerable."[1] This is especially true for how we spend our philanthropic money. Philanthropic and charitable endeavors are imbued with morality whether we like it, acknowledge it, or not.

The more we can remember that money, while a serious tool and a necessity for most of us, is also a complete fantasy, the easier it is to have difficult discussions around it. Let's be intentional about how we earn, save, and deploy it, but let's not get too bogged down by fetishizing, hoarding, or getting too personally laden by our feelings around it. Hopefully, we can lean into greater transparency and generosity around money, too.

One of my favorite activities to get a group ready for brainstorming is the dollar bill game. My Radiant Strategies team did it recently with a group of delightful people who work at a large, global foundation. Folks sat in small groups, and we handed each group a dollar bill. The challenge was to spend three minutes brainstorming uses for the dollar bill that were not currency. It involved examining, handling, folding, waving around, and reimagining the dollar bill. The ideas were all over the map: sunshade, a small fan, use it for note paper (like to make a grocery list), a bookmark, or a blanket for a small animal. Rip it up and it becomes a trail or gerbil bedding. Fold it and it becomes a tent or an accordion, or origami it into a frog, basket, or that fortune teller paku-paku game. Stick it in a time capsule or bottle, write a love note, or have it be the first clue in a long, winding mystery game.

I did it for fun with my family over Thanksgiving. Here's what they came up with:

Snort cocaine (surprisingly, my mother-in-law's idea)
Burn it for fire starter
Screw holder, like for an IKEA project
Toilet paper
"We Love George" fan club for George Washington
A funnel or straw or snorkel

Pin dot for looking at a solar eclipse, a pinhole camera
Cut it into strips and weave a small basket or a small rope
Ruler, a tool to measure things because they're six inches
    long, or to make a right angle
Paper-cut weapon
Wallpaper or floor paper
A lining for a coat or shoes to keep the cold out, moleskin
    like for a blister
If you had to, you could eat it

A little levity, some playful energy, can help keep money in perspective.

It is fascinating to map how money, wealth, generosity, and scarcity move in family systems. I went to social work graduate school, and clinicians of all kinds use genograms as a tool to trace patterns in families. It's a great tool for people working in philanthropy because wealth often resides in and moves through family systems and can be helped or hindered by factors like gender, birth order, education, mental illness or substance abuse, and so on. For example, in my husband's family, to "get" the money, it helped to be born a boy, go to Yale for college, become a banker, and marry a girl born into a wealthy family. To be born a girl, not go to Yale (unavailable to girls before 1969), be gay, be a "black sheep" in some way—these attributes helped you *not* get the money in this family system.

Gender historically has been one of the most important determinants of wealth. For women especially, it is critical to talk about money. In some of our cultures, girls were told to "marry the money and the love will follow." Other women *are* the money, their marriages a matter of dowries, the exchange of land, or an advantageous corporate alliance. Folks born into wealthier families are often warned to "not touch the capital" because that "nut" is the prized possession that preserves the family's wealth, prestige, and social class. And of course, "don't touch the capital" assumes another cast entirely when you consider the prerequisite that marriageable girls be virgins.

In what is shaping up to be a tsunami-size shift, we are in the midst of a huge, generational transfer of wealth that will move trillions of dollars from the Silent Generation and Baby Boomers to women and their heirs. Women control a third of total U.S. household financial assets today—more than $10 trillion. By 2035, women in the United States are projected to control much of the $30 trillion in financial assets that older generations currently possess and will pass on, controlling two-thirds of the wealth in the United States.[2]

Interestingly, across the United States, giving circles are mostly composed of women.

For many of us growing up, talking about money was a serious taboo. For giving circle members, it's imperative that folks talk honestly and openly about money to settle on a set of norms to guide their giving. For many, this may feel even harder than having open conversations around values. If we don't have money, we're told it's rude and grasping to talk about it. If we do have money, we're taught not to brag about it—or even fear that we might be taken advantage of if we make our wealth known. But at the end of the day, we all would do well to realize that not talking about money does not serve us—especially those of us who are trying to shift and disrupt established structures of privilege and power. If you know anything about pay inequality, you know that transparency and communication around salaries is pivotal in correcting wage gaps that disadvantage women and folks of color. The same is true here: the next step to making change is being clear about what we're working with. And one of the biggest tools in a giving circle's toolbox is money.

SEIJI CARPENTER is one of those people who has probably always been cool, but not in that distant cooler-than-you way, more in an "I wanna be your friend," emotionally warm way. He sports white glasses, dark jeans, and often wears his hair partially shaved and up in a bun. I keep honeybees on my roof and he's a regular customer. He grew up in Berkeley, California, with parents who were a doctor and a nurse and also activists; he grew up in a milieu that was socially engaged, socially conscious, and had a "can do" kind of attitude. He's now a Brooklynite and a newish dad and started a giving circle called the Radfund.

Like many folks, Seiji got his political wake-up in college. He was active in Students Against Sweatshops, whose goal was to get Northwestern University to sign on to a workers' consortium, a pledge of sorts that the university's purchased clothing would be made under certain conditions.

Seiji told me, "Now it seems kind of small, in a way, but then, it felt like a lot was riding on it. We felt we had so little power. It was easy for the administration to dismiss us and it was easy to feel discouraged. I remember having endless debates about strategy and tactics, about how powerful we actually were, and what we might accomplish. Some of us were closer to giving up, or making compromises, or accepting a longer timeline, which were the concessions the administration wanted. Some of us felt like we could win. We had a big fight about whether or not to do a sit-in. It was right before Christmas break. It would have been easy to say let's just come back in the spring and decide. Some of the more aggressive folks were like, no, we can't take our foot off the pedal. I was kind of like the swing voter. Ultimately, the group decided to move forward with the sit-in. The day before, the administration gave in and gave us everything we wanted. My assumption was that they got wind of it, but to this day, I don't know how. Most of that group are still friends to this day and I can't see any of them being an administration 'plant'... My take-away is that we did have power. We did get powerful billionaires to do something they didn't want to do. You can strategize and make the best, biggest plans in the world and have all the pieces lined up 'right'—but persistence matters more than any of the particular plays. We kept chipping and chipping and chipping, and eventually, it fell. We had so many debates about which action we should take, which action we should prioritize. In retrospect, they were all good actions. Three bad actions might've been better than two good ones. You can't do it hard and fast for two years, then you win it all. It's a marathon. Make a few calls, now, a few calls then, do a walk-out. How you show up over time is more important than any one thing you might do, any one moment, any one action. The most important thing is to keep at it."

When Seiji moved to Brooklyn ten years ago, he wanted to immerse himself in his new city. And he wanted to stay connected to his organizing roots but didn't have the time and energy he did as a twenty-year-old. He talked with a friend, Helen, who worked at the North Star Foundation. Mario Lugay was a big influence, and through Mario, a dear friend of both of ours, Seiji met me. Seiji says, "Collective giving to us is how we can marry our desire to support movements and engage in movements, with our life-style as working people and, for some of us, new parents. We want to do things that are fun, have joy, are social, and feel collective in powerful ways, and also in fun and silly ways." Radfund's web-site describes them this way: "Radfund is a giving circle based in

Brooklyn, NY. We are a group of friends united by our love of dancing and a commitment to liberation. We give money to folks in NYC organizing to challenge structural inequality and to fight for racial and economic justice."

Seiji and his Radfund collaborators wanted to support organizing in Brooklyn, and they wanted to come up with a financial model that seemed fair and that fit their values. They wanted to retain their identity as a group of friends, while also acknowledging that while they were all well-educated, they were a pretty class-diverse group. They were social workers, education folks, people in tech, and lawyers. They wanted to give in a way that felt like they each had "skin in the game," that felt somehow commensurate. Members who had more economic power should contribute more than those who had less, so their goal was for folks to contribute proportionally to their economic power. And income and wealth were the easiest ways to measure that.

Seiji and another member were more quantitative-minded, so they devised something they call "Formula One." Members would strive to give 1 percent of their income and 0.1 percent of their wealth, and that percentage would rise as income and wealth rose. So, for example, on the income side, each member challenges themselves to give annually at least 1 percent of their annual income, and 2 percent of income over $100,000, 3 percent of income over $200,000, and so on. On the wealth side, members strive to give at least 0.1 percent of their total wealth, and 0.2 percent of wealth over $1 million, 0.3 percent of wealth over $2 million, and so on.

Doing Formula One with a friend group is hard. It requires sharing incomes and wealth with friends. Seiji said it still feels "really naked, really raw." The first time they did it, they didn't approach it with the sensitivity required. Radfund members shared, via email, a Google spreadsheet. Everyone put in their numbers while sitting alone in their apartments. Seiji described it with a wry smile, "We all sat in different rooms and then we all sat in our feelings . . . We are friends! We go to events, art openings together. We go dancing together. Some of us make $50,000 per year, others $500,000 . . . And yeah, it feels kinda shitty to be the one making $50,000. All skills are not valued equally." One member divulged that she has $2 million in a trust fund that no one else knew about. She felt just terrible writing it on a spreadsheet. And everyone else felt terrible just seeing it.

So now they get together to do Formula One in person and talk about the context around the money. One member recently bought an apartment and is more asset rich but currently cash poor. Another member got a big raise, so can do more this year. Or someone just had a kid or someone is still paying off college loans. Seiji said, "There's a story around the number, and since we do it in person, it feels more communal."

They're deliberate and thoughtful about all the extenuating circumstances. Folks put in their wealth, income, and circumstances. Formula One calculates an expected contribution. Then people say what they're actually going to give—sometimes more, sometimes less. Formula One produces an expectation, not a mandatory number. As Seiji describes their system, "We make the numbers and expectations kind of 'hard,' but we are 'soft' on enforcement." It is ultimately a trust-based system.

All in all, Seiji really likes Formula One. It was painful the first time, but the group has gotten better at doing it. It feels fair. Some members of Radfund work in nonprofits and in movements so they don't contribute as much in money, but they contribute so much in terms of information, landscape knowledge of the field, and their perspective as a person who doesn't make a ton of money. Radfund's financial model is hard, and it's not for everyone. Having a pre-existing group of friends with strong relationships with each other is important for this model to succeed.

Radfund is quite exemplary. The way they move their money reflects their values, and Formula One is an expression of their group ethos. Think about the gulf between the member who earns $50,000 per year and the member who earns $500,000 per year. Think about the chasm between the member who has a trust fund and the rest of them who do not. Navigating those gulfs must sometimes feel insurmountable. But they created Formula One to help them cross it.

Within the microcosm that is Radfund, these friends and neighbors are evening out the generational wealth gap. By using a proportional formula that weighs both income and wealth, they've devised a system that feels just. Plus they're having fun together, going to local bars and dance clubs (they call them RadHangs), while doing good in their community. They worked through the natural sad and awkward feelings to create a bigger We together.

And like most giving circles, their impact goes far beyond their money. Radfund also builds connection within its community of grantee partners. Each member of the Radfund becomes the contact person for one grantee partner organization. Seiji told me about one of his favorite pairings. H.O.L.L.A! is a small nonprofit in the Bedford-Stuyvesant (Bed-Stuy) neighborhood of Brooklyn where many of the Radfund members live. H.O.L.L.A! stands for How Our Lives Link Altogether! It's a group for young Black folks from the neighborhood who learn organizing, history, and healing via music, film, and the arts. They put on fun things like talent shows to add vibrancy and connection without a lot of the "at-risk youth" messaging that is so common.

Doug is the Radfund member who is the primary contact person for H.O.L.L.A.! He grew up in humble circumstances and ended up going to business school and now works at a large insurance company. He's pretty conservative in his work life, but a bit of a leftie in his values. Doug met Seiji on a literal dance floor. He'd never taken action in order to make change before and often will not even vote because he's so disillusioned with our political system. But Doug has been transformed by his decade-long relationship with H.O.L.L.A.! and its executive director, Cory Greene. Doug is in his early fifties and white; Cory is Black and now in his thirties. They both live in Bed-Stuy. They watch basketball together. They talk regularly, and what started as a quasi-work relationship has now become a friendship. Seiji has seen the transformation that has blossomed over the last ten years.

To Seiji, this pairing exemplifies the beauty and power of giving circles. Radfund created a bridge for these two men to forge a connection that has transformed them both, which might not have been otherwise possible. Giving circles are closer to people and communities than most formal philanthropies can or try to be. Doug and Cory have transcended the more typical transactive relationship between "doers and donors" (to borrow a phrase from my friend and colleague Stephanie Gillis), and it was a giving circle that created the space for them to start.

MONEY'S HIGHEST AND best use is when it flows. The flow can go toward buying an apartment, investing in a start-up company, or paying for a child to go to college. Philanthropically, money's highest and best use is to flow based on the community's needs.

Money that flows philanthropically can be a source of great pride, power, and legacy building. For so many donors of color

I interviewed, their legacy had been stolen from them. They might be descendants of enslaved people captured and brought over from the African continent; they might be refugees who fled wars abroad; they might be folks whose ancestors migrated north in order to flee a Jim Crow South; a few were descendants of Indigenous people who had been forcibly removed from their ancestral homelands. They had to uproot and come to a new place, often with very little or nothing to connect them with their generational roots.

Moving from Me to We is about articulating ourselves in that space between our ancestors and our heirs. We are the generation that will connect our families' past with our collective futures. For these individuals, the idea of creating one's legacy was especially poignant. Philanthropy is one way of creating legacy on this land—and regardless of our backgrounds or identities, this can be extremely meaningful work for ourselves, our families, and our communities. Building financial capital on behalf of causes we care about is a powerful legacy to leave behind. Building relationships with people is another. Giving circles offer a path for us to do both of these things at once.

Giving circle members give a lot more than their money. We tend to volunteer more, vote more, and are generally more engaged in our communities. In the 2024 landscape study *In Abundance*, the researchers found that 63 percent of members reported an increase in the amount they donate, both within and beyond their collective giving group, since joining. Similarly, 60 percent reported an increase in the amount of time volunteered, including involvement in board service, and in other nonmonetary forms of support for their communities. Additionally, 60 percent indicated a heightened frequency of giving and/or fundraising to support nonprofit organizations and community initiatives.[3]

The Women Donors Network (WDN) is a network of wealthy women who care about gender equity. They organize lobby days to state capitals and, every couple years, to Washington, DC. On one lobby day, a member had arranged to have a fifteen-minute meeting with her state representative. She was a big donor to that rep's campaign, so was granted the request. She brought along the executive director of a nonprofit who had been trying to get a meeting with the representative. After brief introductions, the donor ceded her time to the executive director. What a great way of using one's ties and influence to support a cause and organization you believe in. Individual donors, as opposed to foundations and other institutional donors, have more tools to bring to the social-change party. They can bring their money, for sure, but they can also bring their time, talents, testimony, and ties. They bring their full selves, including their ideas, passions, and networks.

The Asian American Impact Fund is a giving circle in the tristate New York City area that pools its money to fund one organization per year. The chosen organization benefits from the networks and skills of all of the fund's members. So if there's a member who is a fundraiser for a nonprofit, she might help the group create a major donor fundraising plan. And if there's another member who designs websites, they might do a refresh for that year's organization. The Asian American Impact Fund finds that adding their skills and talents to the grantmaking "pot" is another way to build community by helping local nonprofits thrive.

GIVING CIRCLES ARE by their nature a collective effort, so they are intrinsically different from one individual wealthy person giving. In order to make decisions as a group, the group has to talk, discuss, argue, disagree, and, ultimately, decide. It's a democratic form from the outset. And because giving circles collect resources, they cultivate a mindset and practice of sharing for the greater good, moving from silence to talking and from scarcity and hoarding to abundance and generosity. Giving circles invite us to shift our understanding of money from something that is held individually to a community resource. Building a giving circle practice gets the money flowing so it can become a force for good in our communities. And because giving circle members almost always do more than give their money, they perform a kind of alchemy wherein one plus one equals way more than two.

One of the most beautiful things about a giving circle is that it can be as informal as a group of friends doing good together. There is zero need to re-create "formal" philanthropy. In fact, the beauty of doing your giving this way is that you can be unhindered by all that! We, as giving circles, can create what we want. We are not beholden to any corporate structure or any now-deceased founding benefactor. If you want to gather monthly and write checks to a different organization every month, you can do that. If you want to pool money and give once a year to a voted-upon organization, you can do that. You can pool your money and give it to individuals who are not 501(c)(3) charitable organizations— go you! You can pool your money to support political candidates or causes—yay!

Gather friends, talk with each other about what's most important to each person and to your shared community. Then keep the "apparatus" as simple as possible in order to move the group's time, talent, treasure, testimony, and ties into the community.

7

Start Small, Go Big

Micah is a housing attorney, husband, and adorably doting dad to two little kids. He inherited a fortune from his grandfather, and he's a bit uneasy with his wealth, enough so that many of his colleagues and friends don't know about it. He grew up in the northern Midwest in a family with generational loyalty to the Republican party. He's a man of deep Christian faith. This is a guy who is accustomed to being able to figure things out. He has a strong moral compass and a deep desire to do the right thing. Micah is decent and principled, someone who would be a good neighbor, someone who you'd want to have that extra set of your house keys. He believes that every human is entitled to safe, secure, and affordable housing and that housing is a fundamental and basic human need and right. He understands that homelessness is connected, often, to other issues like mental health, substance abuse, joblessness, and so on. But often, it's also primarily about more affordable housing and more access to it. A study out in 2023 by the University of California, San Francisco, surveyed thousands and interviewed hundreds of homeless people in the state. The researchers found that for most of the participants, the cost of housing had simply become too great, and that a rental subsidy or one-time financial aid would have *prevented* their homelessness.[1] So yes, homelessness is connected to many other issues, but primarily, it is a result of the lack of affordable housing.

Micah has dedicated his professional life to this issue by working in housing law, volunteering for organizations that work with homeless folks and advocate for more affordable housing, and moving his philanthropic dollars toward those causes. He knows as much about homelessness and affordable housing as almost anyone, yet he's always felt deeply uncomfortable that people sometimes look to him as a leader in his town on this issue because he's a wealthy donor. He has come to appreciate that he is not an expert on homelessness. In fact, he has said that it is a relief to divest himself of that burden, as it's always felt inauthentic to him. Rather, it is the people who work closely with unhoused folks, and unhoused folks themselves, who know the most about what homeless people might want and need. Hand in hand with policy experts, advocates and lawyers, and people who know how government works, this type of team or coalition can make change happen.

Imagine an alternative Micah who says something like, "I've studied this issue from every angle. I've met with top researchers and served on boards. I should run the organization (or think tank). I will direct the organization to do what I think is best because I'm the expert. Or better yet, I will start an organization that will bring together the best and brightest to solve this issue." This would be Micah being Big Phil. He and his team would come up with lengthy strategic plans, clever logic models, and convoluted performance indicators and raise millions of dollars to increase his impact. Woe to actual experts, the nonprofits on the ground, and unhoused folks themselves who will trip over themselves to please him and most likely see very little benefit.

Imagine another alternative Micah. This Micah says some version of "OMG, homelessness is just too big. It is connected to mental illness, substance abuse, fentanyl and opioids, domestic violence, trafficking, war veterans' services, racism, access to education, immigration policy . . . It's too much, too overwhelming. What can I possibly do as one, albeit wealthy, individual?" So this Micah might get paralyzed in a doom loop of neverending learning, guilt, and feelings of powerlessness.

Yes, homelessness is an incredibly complex issue. Yes, it can be overwhelming. And undeniably it will necessitate a combination of solutions: building more affordable housing, connecting people to services for that whole long list of other needs, and much more. But everyone must start somewhere. Otherwise, what is the alternative? To do nothing.

Tackling homelessness in its an entirety would be a daunting task for an entire government, let alone a single individual. Micah has bit off a chunk of this problem that is doable for him, right now. That means he focuses on his hometown and a U.S.-based context for city, state, and national policy. He stays informed via work, reading, attending conferences, and volunteering. He is grounded in his faith and his family. He is learning that he occupies two or three seats around the social change table—for him, that might be donor plus board member plus attorney. But there are many other seats around that table for whom Micah is a support person and colleague, like the people who run organizations, march and protest, lobby in state capitols, do direct service work, run policy think tanks, do research at universities, and so on. Micah started with *one* action and has gone on to have a large impact on his community.

When the AWGC was still getting off the ground, we began to think about some of the logistics, such as how much we should give and raise, where we should direct our efforts, what the process might be—and it sometimes felt too big, like how could we even begin to make a dent? We were bubbling with excitement, but New York City is huge. There are hundreds of Asian American identities, ethnicities, languages, and cultures represented within the five boroughs of our city. I mean just eating different cuisines along the 7 train through Queens could take decades! Every cause is valid and seems urgent—services for new immigrants, programs for women and girls, antiviolence, antipoverty, mental health, the criminal justice system, access to education, access to healthcare—oh my goodness, how were we ever going to decide which cause to support let alone take meaningful action?

IT SEEMS COUNTERINTUITIVE, but even we humans who want to help manage to create barriers to giving away our money charitably. Giving circles can get stuck here, too. Giving circle organizers can get overwhelmed by trying to do too much and also sometimes by the sheer scale of the problems we face. For people who are trying to organize and move money, the feeling of overwhelm can show up in many ways.

"We don't have enough money."

"We don't know enough about this issue. And this issue is huge."

Or "The amount of money we can raise is dwarfed by the scale of the thing we are trying to address."

Like feeling overwhelmed, perfectionism can also be a barrier to action. "We can't do this unless we do it right." I know a very nice, earnest, supersmart, rather technocratic woman who works for a large U.S.-based foundation in New York City. On their five-year anniversaries, employees get to give a grant that matches their anniversary date of hire. So upon five years' tenure, you get to give $5,000 to a charity of your choice, upon ten years, it's $10,000, and so on. Mikaela celebrated her twentieth year working at the foundation, so she has $20,000 to give to any nonprofit organization in the United States. Pretty cool, right? Mikaela is a senior program director, and because of her family circumstances, she's pretty wealthy in her own right. For over a year now, Mikaela hasn't been able to decide where to direct her $20,000. She is bound up in the perfection trap. She works in philanthropy, so she is inundated with all the "best" solutions and most recent data. She might feel an extra burden of doing it "right" because she is in leadership. She feels like she doesn't want to "waste" this amazing opportunity, so she's got to pick the "best" organization. And she's deeply enmeshed in a technocratic mindset, which can tend to clog up the flow of dollars. People, giving circles, and institutions can all suffer occasionally from constipation.

I imagine there might be a small battle going on in Mikaela's head. Think of that old meme of an angel on one shoulder and a devil on the other. In her heart, Mikaela might really want to donate the $20,000 to her kids' private school's capital campaign. It's been an amazing place for her two children to learn, grow, and experiment. They're on the cutting edge of pedagogy, and she's on the school's capital campaign committee. Or she might truly want to donate it to her daughter's lacrosse team, which has an outreach program for underserved children in her town. But if she's being honest with herself, Mikaela knows that her donation will also help her own, already quite privileged child. She's stuck between wanting to do the "right" thing and what she'd really prefer to do but can't because of optics. And she's having a hard time discerning what the "right" thing is in the first place because she's stuck on metrics and on finding the best, most perfect organization.

Wobbly values can make one wobbly on decision-making, too. It is possible Mikaela can't decide how to spend her charitable dollars because she can't say out loud what her values are. For Mikaela in this case, she might be afraid of saying it out loud because it might be "my kids *even over* all kids."

To Mikaela I would say: give to your kids' school and to your daughter's lacrosse team. They've both been awesome places for your family and your children's learning and social-emotional development, and other children will benefit, too. Acknowledge the self-interest as an acceptable compromise. But don't stop there! You've got so many resources at your disposal, way beyond the $20,000 from your workplace this year. Consider the $20,000 bump something of a challenge. Make a commitment to match it by augmenting your family's usual charitable giving this year; add time, talent, testimony, and ties to that treasure. Expand the table to include organizations that provide similar benefits to families unlike your own. Talk about it with your colleagues. This is a real-life case study that all donors, whether they give $5 or $5 million, face. I'm confident the team will appreciate your candor as a leader and the opportunity to talk about these issues. And I guarantee you will learn something from engaging in the debate with them, and that will inform what you do five years from now when you've got $25,000 to give!

Being overwhelmed can also show up as overthinking. Several years ago a friend of a friend called me as she was starting an Asian American giving circle in Boston. She and her group wanted to raise money in support of organizations serving the

Asian American population in the region, and the circle would be composed of Asian American people across many different ethnicities and cultures, similar to the AWGC. The group was totally frozen on this one nagging thing. They couldn't get past it and it was clogging up their nascent project before it had even begun! Should they take money from white friends, colleagues, families?

The answer is yes. Take money from white people. The decision-makers and the grantee partners will be Asian American people and organizations. So you're good to go.

The main goal and value here is sending resources to under-resourced Asian American communities in Boston. There are some funding sources that might present challenges from a values perspective, like maybe the group wouldn't accept donations from a company that makes pesticides that are ruining groundwater in rural India. But accepting money from friends and families of giving circle members, even the ones who aren't Asian, is fine!

"We don't know enough" and its cousin, "this issue is just too huge" constantly rear their gnarly heads in the world of philanthropy. The many issues we face, as families, neighborhoods, cities, and nationally, are huge, systemic, and can definitely feel overwhelming. All this may lead to hesitation and overthinking, but the answer is usually to take a deep breath and start small.[2]

I admire Micah and many of the others in this book because they are doing something, even small, local actions. Micah has figured out that although he knows a lot about homelessness and affordable housing, there are people who work in the field day in and day out who know a lot more. Learning is good (and ideally, a lifelong endeavor!), but action matters a whole lot. It's not sequential—you don't need to wait until you're an expert to do something about it.

. . .

SO HOW DID we women of the Asian Women Giving Circle get over our feelings of overwhelm? That fear and worry that we were so small, what good could possibly come from our small dollars? How could we possibly learn enough to make good grants? We live in a vast city—what was the right-size first step for us? Who were the other Asian American funders? We didn't want to step on any toes, and we wanted to be additive to the space.

To fight the overambition and overwhelm, we figured out a niche that spoke to us in a meaningful, personal, and specific way. Funding narrative and culture change fit us because some of us are also artists, we are all culture fans, and we all believe deeply that culture change leads to political and social change. Finding our niche also helped carve out a spot within the crowded and big philanthropic sector in New York City. We've been pleased to see bigger, national funders now jumping into the cultural and narrative change space. Nothing makes us happier than to see a grantee partner leverage our $5,000 or $8,000 grant into a $50,000 or $150,000 grant from the Ms. Foundation for Women, the Ford Foundation, or the Sundance Institute Documentary Fund. We feel like proud mamas and aunties every time. We're chuffed to have been early proponents and funders of artist activists, and we're delighted to have been a small part of the amazing work we've been able to support. Check out the work of Muslim American comedian Negin Farsad, Korean American artist Chang-Jin Lee, Korean Palestinian activist and leader Suhad Babaa (Just Vision), spoken word provocateur performer Kate Rigg a.k.a. Lady K-Sian and Slanty Eyed Mama, Indo-Caribbean artist activist Taij Kumarie Moteelall, and the organizations Kundiman, Asian American Writers' Workshop, Jahajee, W.O.W. Project, and so many more.[3]

To counter the perfectionism barrier, we give each other grace. We are a group of women who have lives made busy with all the things—work, family, kids, aging parents, partners. A few years in, my friend and AWGC member BJ called. She was expecting twins. I knew I wouldn't see her for a few years, or maybe ten. But I also knew I could call her if we needed a sound, sane, opinion (plus she's a lawyer). Or if we needed some cool music for an event (she and her brother are music producers on the side). We've managed to create a group culture that is accepting of the ebbs and flows of life that happen when jobs are gained and lost, kids are born and go to school, parents age and die, partnerships and marriages begin, bobble, or end. When one member lost her job, we let her contribution requirement slide that year, and some of us chipped in more to make up the difference. We're not a punitive bunch. We aim to keep our vibe collegial, even sisterly. And we're doing work rooted in our values and our community, which steadies us to give each other time, space, understanding, food and succor, a shoulder to cry on, a high-five, a commiserating phone call, a knowing look, community, love—all of which add up to grace.

To beat back the "we don't have enough money" worry, the short answer is, yes, you do! In our case, every dollar we raise and give is a dollar that would not have been raised nor given. There is so little organized philanthropy by and for Asian Americans, and a tiny fraction of that is steered toward women, girls, and gender-expansive folks. So our pot helps. There is so little money going to culture and narrative change as a strategy for social change that our body of work has made a real difference, especially for Asian American artist activists.

Sometimes $4,000—or even $400—can be enough. Even in the face of enormous problems, what feels like a drop in the bucket is so, so, so much more than that. It's a shot in the arm, a vote of confidence, the feeling that someone believes in you. It's comradery and the feeling that we're all in this together.

Also—it's more than just the money, honey. Money is important for sure, and moving money toward community organizations doing great work is critical. But we as individuals living in those communities can do, and do, so much *more* than donate dollars. We buy things, hire people, and vote. Some of us invest money. These activities are all ways in which to move values in the world. Giving charitable dollars is only a tiny fraction of the dollars (and attitudes) we can move and influence.

IT WAS ONE of those glorious, bright blue, crisp cold winter days in New York City. The Asian Women Giving Circle had made a tiny grant to Q-Wave, a group of scrappy, young, Asian American activists and organizers who wanted to integrate the official Chinatown Lunar New Year Parade to include gay, queer, and trans people. It was 2009, and at that time, queer folks were not allowed to be out and march in the Parade. Q-Wave had applied for a $4,000 grant so they could crash the party with a visual spectacle of rainbow flags, dragon kits, and flying fish. We women of the AWGC were excited to fund their project and march alongside them—official sanction or not. Our $4,000 was the only grant they had, and it paid for beer, Oreos, and art supplies. The night before the parade, Q-Wave received official permission to march, and the next day, we walked together in jubilation. That night as my husband and I made dinner for our kids, I heard Q-Wave organizers interviewed on WNYC, my local NPR affiliate. They were covered in the *New York Times* and *Time Out New York*. At the time, the St. Patrick's Day Parade still barred openly queer participants, but from that year forward, the Chinatown Lunar New Year Parade would be open to all. They'd made history.

I love this story so much because it demonstrates what a group of scrappy, young activists can accomplish with a ton of heart and not a ton of money. And it demonstrates that a group of scrappy philanthropists can stand alongside and make history with them. We've gone on to partner with Q-Wave on several more projects, and we've now funded well over one hundred amazing artists and organizations in New York City. Our grantee partners have told us that we are often their only funder who is not a blood relative. We are almost always the only funder who looks like them.

Q-Wave integrating the Chinatown Lunar New Year Parade is such a great example of cultural change (which can feel kind of nebulous) and how important it is. Queer people out and marching in that most public and celebratory of ways is like the genie in the bottle; once out, that genie is not going back inside. Remember when Ellen DeGeneres came out on TV, and *Modern Family* introduced gay characters into America's living rooms every week? Q-Wave broke through that barrier for Asian Americans in New York City and for Chinese Americans in Chinatown. And since that day, LGBTQ+ folks can be out, proud, and march on Lunar New Year.

It's also such a great example of small dollars helping to make big change. Our $4,000 grant helped Q-Wave make history. Don't underestimate yourself, your giving circle, or the projects you'll fund. Be open to the surprise and the possibility of making history, too.

Q-Wave changed New York City forever for gay Asian Americans. Though their grant-ask was small, their vision was huge. They approached their transformative project with optimism, comradery, humor, flags and puppets, imagination, and a strong sense of being on the right side of history. They didn't let overwhelm, perfectionism, or any of the million worries that can get in the way of making social change stop them.

Lily Messing was a sophomore in high school when she had her big idea. She started with ten kids from ten different high schools in Tucson, Arizona, to get started. She launched 100+ Teens Who Care, modeled after a giving circle network called 100+ Women Who Care. Lily's circle eventually grew to 180 students who each gave $25 per quarter. Students pitched non-profits and the full group voted. Their first year, the kids raised and gave away $13,000 to two youth-serving organizations and a cat shelter. Lily was interviewed in a local paper when she won the Outstanding Youth in Philanthropy award in 2022: "I strongly feel that regardless of age, one should be able to influence their community positively. By oneself, a $25 donation to charity does not seem like it will make much of an impact. But when you combine that $25 with the donations of 100-plus like-minded teens, we can create real change in our community."[4] Lily has been recruited as a youth philanthropy coach to help set up 100+ Teens Who Care in several cities across the United States. There are now fifteen chapters around the country and counting.[5]

I love Lily and her friends' can-do, community-minded spirit. I'm sure there were naysayers and the usual doubts about scale, money, overwhelm, complex issues, and so on. But Lily and her friends jumped in. They are doing a pro-social thing, a social good. Their first year, they raised $13,000 in a collective manner that hadn't been raised or given before. They organized across different high schools in their city. They researched and pitched nonprofits to each other, probably did some haggling and persuading, then they organized a democratic process and voted. They learned more about organizations, causes, and issues in their city that are important to their peers. They had values-based conversations with other high school students. They felt the comradery that comes from shared purpose. They got the mental health boost from doing something and feeling like they had efficacy. I would bet they also volunteered more, and they'll be more likely to vote.

And they're kids! As they move on in their lives, some of them will continue learning, seeking, and asking why. They will observe and experience the connections between the on-the-ground social services of the type they've supported via 100+ Teens Who Care and the more "upstream" reasons those social services are needed in the first place.

I met a woman years ago who started a giving circle at work. Every two weeks on payday, she and her colleagues would put $20 into their collective giving pot. Every few months, they'd get together over lunch at work and decide where to give their collected money. They met in the staff break room or at the literal water cooler. They kept it simple: collect the money, discuss over lunch, send the money. They took a structure that already existed—colleagues, meeting casually during lunch break, workplace friendships and rhythms—and turned it into something more.

Small change? Maybe. But all these small changes circle up to big change, collectively.

. . .

PETER AND I raised our three kids in New York City. We walked to the West Village Nursery School on Horatio Street in the then-gritty Meatpacking District where you could still smell carcasses on hooks and see blood on the streets. Wigs, heels, ripped lingerie, and condoms littered our walk because the Meatpacking District was that kind of market, too.

Now, the Meatpacking District is full of expensive restaurants, posh boutiques, and glitzy flagships for international brands like Hermès, Diane von Furstenberg, Christian Louboutin, and Louis Vuitton. To the designer replacements, our West Village block lost our neighborhood pet store, bookstore, two bodegas, a record store, and a sweet funky bead store run by a bent older gentleman who loved cats.

As the West Village changed, the inhabitants got a lot wealthier. When we moved in, our co-op apartment building was full of teachers, artists, film and music people, journalists and writers, and a few lawyers. As they retired, died, or moved on, the building filled up with younger, richer people. It seemed like overnight that our kids' school went from do-it-yourself potluck fundraisers to big, themed auction nights that raised hundreds of thousands of dollars. I used to donate a Korean cooking lesson/dinner at our place until finally, after several years, the couple who bought it came over, treated me like their personal chef/servant, and the guy eventually asked for a steak instead (because he didn't like garlic, as in hello! Korean cooking at Hali and Peter's house?!). Obviously for this guy, dinner was less about sharing than it was about serving. Something precious got lost in the transition from potlucks to catered galas. The school might have raised more money, but it lost some of its soul.

I've loved raising my kids in New York for lots of reasons, but if I had to pick my least favorite challenge of parenting in this city, it would be avoiding that "race to the top" energy. The parenting culture among the middling to affluent to wealthy subculture in which we lived was achievement oriented and competitive. People really did pull all the strings they could to get into the right preschool that would feed into the right private school that would feed into an Ivy League college. People moved to get into the right zip code for the best public schools. They hired psychologists, educational consultants, and lawyers to get their kids extra time on standardized tests.

We didn't always succeed, but Peter and I tried our best to *not* enter that race. Amy Chua's book *Battle Hymn of the Tiger Mother* came out when my kids were school-age and, geez, what a giant step backward for Asian American parents. Most Americans already have stereotypes about Asian Americans, such as that we're naturally good at standardized tests, that we are genetically engineered for engineering, that we are kind of robotic, pliant, and good cogs in large machines. Well-meaning mom friends (all white women) have said to me things like, "Of course your kid did well at school because you're a Tiger Mom." Not only does that flatten me (I'm actually more like a Golden Retriever Mom, as some of my Asian American mom friends have teased me), but even more enraging, statements like that strip agency from my kids.

Rather than top-of-the-jungle, apex-predator types, Peter and I tried to be "good-enough" parents. D. W. Winnicott was an English pediatrician and psychologist who coined the phrase "the good-enough mother" in 1953.[6] I wish he had included fathers and all parents in his writing, but the idea is that to raise psychologically healthy kids who feel nurtured and loved, you don't have to be the best parent, or a perfect one, but simply good enough. Children don't need perfect parents. In fact, striving for perfection can be bad for children, as they need to learn, over time, to deal with frustration and to fend for themselves. Children need parents who try to meet their needs sensitively and responsively most of the time, even if they are occasionally distracted, grumpy, and imperfect. And they need parents who appreciate and enjoy play.[7]

Writer and teacher Avram Alpert wrote *The Good Enough Life* that expands Winnicott's idea into a whole social order. Competing to be the smartest, richest, most famous benefits no one. Alpert writes that in fact, the hypercompetitive race to the top damages our own health, our relationships, and our planet. Wouldn't it be better if we could work together to create a world that was good enough for all, rather than destroying ourselves in a sum-zero, illusory slog toward fame, wealth, or whatever it is we think we want? Good enough is a more balanced and realistic choice and a necessary antidote to greatness thinking or greatness striving.[8] Toward the end of her review of Alpert's book in *The Atlantic*, Lily Meyer writes, "You don't have to be great to have a good life; you don't have to be a moral genius to live well. All you have to do is be interested, keep your eyes open, and not quit."[9]

"Good enough" is such a useful frame for building a collective giving practice. Rather than letting ourselves be paralyzed by the scope of the problems, or the infinite variations on the "how," or the worry that we might get it wrong, or the illusory quest for the best, get out there and try something. Do one action. Like with parenting, there is no one right way. There are infinite right ways. Good enough is truly good enough, and learning along the way should be one of the group's shared values. The trick is finding a good-enough way forward and staying open to learning—paying attention to what works, what doesn't, and what you might try next time. Stay interested, keep learning, and don't quit.

Starting small does not mean doing little, or setting our sights too low, or tempering our ambitions. Rather, starting small is a way to begin. And it turns out that going small instead of big sometimes ends up being big anyway.

Part III

THE BIG WE

Part II

Building Belonging

L ooking back, I think I started the Asian Women Giving Circle because I wanted Asian American girlfriends. Growing up in Kansas City, I'd never had Asian American besties before.

Inspired by the sisterhood of the New York Women's Foundation where I'd served on the Board of Directors, and several *gehs* with girlfriends, I started the Asian Women Giving Circle in 2005. I realized in one of my girlfriend *gehs* that each of us was giving charitably, but none of us was being all that intentional about it. We might respond to an appealing appeal, or give to a friend's cause, but we'd never, say, decided to focus on women and girls in New York City, or on Asian American families newly immigrated to this country. What would it look like to turn this *geh* idea into a charitably focused pot of money instead? What would it feel like to have conversations with my friends about what mattered most to us, and then decide together, how to move some money?

That first meeting on a warm summer's day, we met in Millie Chan's living room because it was the biggest. Angie was impossibly hugely pregnant, and amazingly, that baby is off to college soon. We were a group of ten that first year—about half worked in nonprofits, about half in finance, publishing, government, and corporate. We were mostly in our thirties to our late fifties. We came from many different Asian American backgrounds and immigration trajectories. We were all well-educated. Some of us were moms, some were partnered, some neither. But we were all so excited to embark on this shared adventure together.

Eighteen years later, the AWGC has become a very beloved community for me, a reliably smart, principled, down-to-earth, honest, straight-talking, hilarious group of women who together make a "home" within our big home of New York City. We've expanded well beyond that initial small friend group. Today we number twenty-five women, ranging in age from our late twenties to our early eighties and across multiple Asian American ethnicities and experiences. We've remained an all-volunteer sisterhood, and to date, we've raised and distributed $1.5 million to Asian American women and gender-expansive artist activists in New York City.

We never intended to grow into a larger organization or be national in scope. We knew we would start with girlfriends, then maybe expand our circles outward while always trying to hold true to the personal connection that encompasses "girlfriends." We knew we'd be all-volunteer; that we'd do our best; that good enough would be good enough; that we'd take time if we needed to for kids, parents, work, life; that we'd keep the overhead/administration light; and that we'd endeavor to have fun while doing good.

When we started, the threads that bound together the women of the Asian Women Giving Circle were fairly coarse and they were few. We were all Asian American women who cared deeply about Asian American women, girls, and gender-expansive folks in New York City. And we soon realized that we believed in the power of culture to seed the ground for social change. We were pretty diverse as regards to age, profession, cultural backgrounds, immigration backgrounds, where we grew up in the United States, and so on. Now, almost twenty years later, the threads that connect us have become finer; our ball of yarn has grown bigger, more varied and complex. Subgroups of us talk, commiserate, listen, and sometimes argue around issues such as raising kids in New York, caring for elderly parents, losing jobs and relationships, gaining jobs and relationships. Some have traveled together; others are regular dinner and movie buddies; others are activist buddies. Sometimes I notice that the Chinese American or Korean American or Bengali American women get together for more specific connections. There's a beautiful interweaving, pulling out, and coming together that happens now that didn't happen in the early days. Our circle has matured and grown more complex. And we feel and are more intertwined.

Andine Sutarjadi is a dear AWGC sister. I feel like I'm one of her New York City aunties. She is in her early thirties, recently married, with celebrations in Indonesia (her family) and in Maine (his) and works in philanthropy. She is just coming "out" as a younger-generation member of a very wealthy family, so she is finding her own path that will forge together her personal and professional identities.

Andine came to the United States for college, to "get as far away from my family as possible. I love them, but they are a lot." She ordered a bunch of college catalogs and chose Boston University, to her mother's horror. The snow! The distance! The boys!

Andine told me, "I come from a place where everyone looks like me. I never thought about what it meant to be a minority. I am indigenous to Indonesia. I speak the language, we have been there for seven, eight generations, maybe more. I'm a Muslim woman. Then I moved to the United States. For the first time, I realized I'm a minority. Oh wow, Islamophobia is real. In Indonesia, we are it. I took it for granted, what is right and what is true."

Andine continued, "In philanthropy, it's even worse! I'm even more of a minority." In 2018, she was working at Women Moving Millions (WMM), a philanthropic network for women who have committed to give at least $1 million to a woman's fund. Her boss, Courtney Harvey, is a Korean adoptee, friend, and colleague. Andine realized she hadn't spent a family holiday at home in ten years. Courtney asked her, "Are you okay? Are you lonely? I think you need to meet Hali. She spoke at the [WMM] Summit last year. Let's go to Hali's house and we can meet her honeybees, and we can hang out. You need family here. You need some aunties in your life." So they came over and we looked in on the bees, had tea, sat around my kitchen table, and talked and talked, laughed, cried, talked some more. And Andine joined the Asian Women Giving Circle.

Two or so years afterward, Andine and another AWGC sister, Chitra Aiyer, cofacilitated a meeting at Pat Kozu's house. Chitra opened the meeting by asking the group to share "what's one really Asian thing you did this weekend?" Everyone said something, like I went to Queens so my mom could use my monthly MetroCard to do a bunch of errands, or I saw this film, or I put kimchi on my eggs. Andine told me, "For some reason, it really resonated with me. This was a lived experience that I could relate to. People talked about motherhood, families, their girlhoods. Someone talked about the history of Asians in the United States. And that was the first time I realized I should learn about that. That was literally the first time I asked myself, 'Am I an immigrant? Am I Asian American?' If I have kids, they would 100 percent be Asian

American. That made me really want to learn and invest more. I resonated with all these ladies' lived experiences. Where you live really does become part of who you are."

At the age of twenty-seven, Andine had found a home within our big city, New York City, a place where she belonged, a place where she is a regular.

Andine is such a regular that she comes over for meetings (and the occasional party) usually with a giant container of Indonesian fried noodles, *mie goreng* (see endnote for the recipe).[1] She and the other sisters of the AWGC bring spare Tupperware for the leftovers. She remembers a meeting in which someone asked, "What's the ailment this month?" Oh, my back has been hurting, or my wrist has a tweak, or I've been having these migraines. Then inevitably, what follows is "try this herb or this tea," or "call my doctor and here's her number." Andine told me, "This is a familial experience. I don't have that here. When I'm in Jakarta, my mom asks, 'How did you sleep?' It's that kind of conversation with the giving circle. I don't have that with my friends or at work. I have that with my husband because I'm training him to be an honorary Asian . . . The Giving Circle feels like a homecoming, honestly . . . I wanted to be far from home. Everyone knows me in Indonesia. Everyone knows my family. I wanted to be somewhere where no one knows who I am. But being so unseen was a shock. The invisibility of being Asian American women in this country is a shock. Being a part of the circle, you are so seen, you are seen times a million, like seen too much, nosy seen. And I love that! I want more of that! Ask me more questions about my life!"

Whether or not they are organized around an identity group or shared experience like ours, collective giving groups foster belonging and connection to community. In the 2024 landscape study, an overwhelming 91 percent of members stated that their participation has positively impacted their sense of belonging.[2] Over the years, even with members cycling in and out, we women of the Asian Women Giving Circle have created long-lasting connections with one another. Creating community and fostering relatedness are obvious antidotes to the epidemic of loneliness that plagues us. But building belonging and community are also the core of creating a bigger We. Fostering deep relationships with one another is the gateway to nurturing a more effective, enduring generosity practice, but even more importantly, it is the foundation of a stronger civil society.

The informality of the AWGC helps us build belonging. Giving circles tend to not have formal application processes, or if they do, they're not too onerous. For the most part, we don't have boards of directors, complex reporting requirements, or require tons of paperwork or letters of recommendation. In the AWGC's case, each of us steering members is pretty easy to get hold of, meaning there are no program officers or other gatekeepers. We try to be responsive when people reach out. There are not layers and layers of people in between us and the projects we fund. We're there because we want to be there and because we care.

Proximity is another community builder. Most giving circles are groups of friends, colleagues, or neighbors who live near one another and fund projects near or in their communities. We are embedded in our communities. It's hard to feel above or apart from each other when you run into one another at restaurants, the park, the farmers' market, or the grocery store. Proximity also means that we can relate to many of the issues the projects we fund are trying to address. For example, when we hear about a project having to do with lack of understanding or knowledge, or outright hostility and banishment for queer kids in many Asian American families, pretty much everyone agrees that is a big issue. We know because it is our families, too. We have funded in this area since our inception.

Chitra is a member of the steering committee today, but she was previously the head of a grantee partner organization. Several of us have led or been board members of organizations that have received funding. In the giving circle neighborhood of philanthropy, the distinction between who we are and who gets funding isn't always black and white. There's always a line between funder and fundee, but it's as if the lines are smudged charcoal rather than permanent ink.

SOMETIMES IT IS those just on the outskirts of belonging who feel most acutely how important it is to feel it. Sometimes it is those on the margins who have the clearest point of view. They can sometimes have the best perspectives to point out what's missing, identify problems, usher in updates, and find relevance, refreshes, even transformations.[3] I'm accustomed to being just on the outside, too. I keenly observe everyone, even as they're often not looking (or listening to, or even noticing I'm there) at me.

One of the very moving lessons I learned from the research I led on donors of color is that even for folks who are highly connected and super well networked, finding belonging can remain elusive. That feeling of being an outsider, always walking around the edges, is so familiar to many of us. Yet we keep trying, searching for those bonds. With the donors of color research and network build, it was beautiful to see the connections that happened across different life experiences. We *can* find each other, and it helps to create or discover vehicles that enable those connections—like giving circles.

Armando Castellano is one of the nicest people I've ever met in philanthropy. I interviewed him for the donors of color research and by the end of that conversation in his living room, we had all laughed, guffawed, cried, and took turns trying out his new La-Z-Boy-style full-body-massager reclining chair. Armando lives in Silicon Valley in a warm, comfortable, animal-filled home; I recall two dogs, more than one cat, a bunny somewhere, lots of plants in a very lush garden, and a big jumble of bikes. He's got two sons and a Dutch wife who is an educator.

Armando was around thirty years old when his dad won the California State Lottery in 2001, and it was, at the time, the largest lottery pot in state history. His father, Alcario (Al), had been working at the local Safeway, and his mom, Carmen, as an executive assistant at a community college. Overnight, his family's socioeconomic situation changed dramatically. He remembers being awakened by the phone call at 6:00 a.m. while in bed with his future wife, and asking her, "What even is the lottery?" His parents had always been very active in their Latino and Mexican American communities, so they naturally moved their winnings into seeding the Castellano Family Foundation. The foundation has since closed ("sunsetted" in philanthropy speak) but it had a big impact on Latino communities in Santa Clara County, moving over $10 million to Latinx leaders and nonprofits.

Armando is a classical French horn player. He is the founder and director of Quinteto Latino, a performance and education organization that performs classical music by Latin American and Latino composers. His early classical music education and training involved playing a pretty exclusively "white male reper-toire,"[4] so his professional work now is a thoughtful antidote to that earlier formal training. Armando told me that he didn't see a person of color horn player until he turned seventeen, adding for emphasis, "and I was looking!"

Armando wears multiple hats and has said of himself, "I'm often the only frickin' one!" meaning he is often the only Chicano or Latino man in a classical music space, or the only Latino man in a philanthropy-sector room or the only wealthy person in a primarily Chicano space. He was the first in his family to fly on a plane. He always had a hard time at school until he found his people via music (he's a self-described "band geek"). He finds it easier to talk about money with white people. He has a love-hate relationship with his affluent, mostly white neighborhood. He told me several years ago, "I hate this neighborhood. They don't talk to me unless I'm with my white wife. It's crazy. They don't even look at me." He gets mistaken for the gardener. He'd like to move to a different, less ostentatious neighborhood when his kids grow up.

When we were building the Donors of Color Network, we did a series of living room conversations around the country. Imagine anywhere from eight to forty people of color, all very wealthy, sitting on sofas and chairs in cities like Dallas, Boulder, Atlanta, Berkeley, Boston, Seattle, and the Upper West Side of Manhattan. We gathered in someone's living room, noshed on food and wine, shared the research and findings to date, shared family and cultural backgrounds, then basically let the conversation flow. Themes included generosity, cultural and familial traditions around giving, stories passed down in families, immigration stories if there were any, ways in which folks volunteered or were engaged civically, faith-based and secular practices around helping others and community building. The people in the living room usually didn't know each other well; they'd been invited by me or were maybe a friend, or a friend of a friend of the host.

On two separate occasions, grown men burst into tears upon entering the rooms. Armando was one of those men. He shared afterward, "Wow. I just didn't know I was missing this until I saw it. I didn't know I needed that room until I experienced it." The people who came to those living room conversations were highly networked via alumni, fraternal, business, professional, and social networks. Yet they were not networked philanthropically, and they were not connected across race, culture, and ethnicity.

Armando's perspective as an outsider, as often "the only frickin' one," gives him a sort of superpower. He sees things from multiple perspectives, and doing so is deeply ingrained. Sure it's sometimes extra labor, but he adds to his already empathetic personality a very thoughtful and humble awareness of being a bridge builder, ambassador, translator—literally and figuratively. I think part of the reason he cried in that room is that it hit him, suddenly, how much he would not have to be in that bridge-building role in that room. How he could almost take a rest.

The rooms we curated in those early days of the Donors of Color Network felt like homes, respites, places where we could see and be seen in our full humanity. Similarly to how I didn't know that deep inside, part of the reason I started the Asian Women Giving Circle was because I had a deep longing to have Asian American girlfriends, for the first time ever. Kind of like Andine didn't know she needed to find an Asian American girlfriend home in her adopted hometown of New York City.

When we found Armando for the donors of color research, he was already super well-connected via his family foundation, his classical music community, his family and friends and kids' schools' communities. But he didn't know he needed a community that was cross-race and composed entirely of people of color who were doing philanthropy. And upon finding it, it hit him so hard he wept. Armando went on to join the inaugural board of directors of the Donors of Color Network. He went on to help create that community that so many of us longed for, that we never even knew we needed.

For Andine and Armando, neither knew they needed the community they found. Finding the Asian Women Giving Circle and the Donors of Color Network filled a need they didn't even know they had. Something magical happens for the group, too. Coming together around shared purpose amplifies the impact of the group such that the collective becomes stronger than the sum of its individual parts. The members of a giving circle bring all their Five T's to the table, plus giving circle members give more money, volunteer more time, vote more often, and get more educated about what's going on in their communities. They have more power because they walk arm in arm with each other.

THE 2024 LANDSCAPE report on collective giving, *In Abundance*, found that a staggering 77 percent of giving circle members reported an uptick in their learning about social injustice through participation in their groups. The researchers write, "This individual-level growth in understanding complements the group-level commitment to equity-driven practices, fostering a holistic approach to addressing societal inequities."[5] Jamie Rasberry, director of policy and strategic partnerships at the Mississippi Alliance of Nonprofits and Philanthropy, talks about the ripple effect of circle members' learning. Let's say the circle raises money to buy backpacks for kids. By digging deeper and deeper into the "why," they soon learn more about the socioeconomics of being a single mom, say, or of being a child who stays at school for many more hours than the school day, about transportation challenges in town, or maybe also the lack of good jobs.

These circle members have gotten to know each other. They've begun to trust each other, and that opens up the possibilities for asking harder questions and learning together. By building belonging, giving circle members can dig deeper into why kids need backpacks. Rather than just buying the backpacks, giving circle members can talk about the larger societal, economic, and even political roots in their communities that comprise the deeper why. Getting to the deeper why builds greater belonging, too, because rather than seeing backpack recipients as "other," members understand that individuals aren't the problem, systems are, and that unites more of us in the social change endeavor. Ultimately, plumbing these depths makes giving circle members better, more engaged, more knowledgeable, and more compassionate philanthropists.

Giving circles are little hotpots of democracy because its members are learning about issues impacting our society, and they have to practice skills like advocating, voting, compromising, sometimes losing, sometimes winning, but always in furtherance of a larger goal. All this circles up to building more civically engaged citizens who care, learn, and act together.

IF YOU'D LIKE it to be diverse, it's really important to build that in from the start.

We all need to practice talking, working, collaborating, and partying with people who are different from us. Some giving circles explicitly bring together people across differences as part of their founding DNA. I met a woman who is starting a giving circle in her large apartment building in Harlem. The members share the same building, but that's about it. A giving circle is a great place to exercise this muscle because it works toward a larger good, there is built-in relationship building, it's volunteer, it's regular but not too much, and it doesn't require any special skills or lots of money.

When we were building the Donors of Color Network, I had some difficult conversations with women who were leading women's philanthropy networks. They complained to me with various versions of "why are you building another network when we have such a good one here? Yes, it's true, our network is mostly white women, but we are working really hard to make it not so. Can't you just bring the women of color you're finding and interviewing over to our place?" These were earnest pleas, borne from frustration. And these women's networks are doing incredible work in the world and are truly trying to diversify their membership, yet they remain, to this day, mostly white.

This is an extremely unpopular finding from the research we did to build the Donors of Color Network. Just like you cannot change who your biological parents and family are, it is very hard to change the founding DNA of an organization. If you start an organization or a network or a giving circle that is mostly wealthy white women who live on the coasts, ten or twenty years later, the majority composition of your network, organization, or giving circle will be white, wealthy women who live on the coasts. The philanthropy networks in the United States today have not been able to meaningfully integrate themselves to include people who are unlike the founders. Change is happening, but it feels glacial. The reasons are complex, but two big factors inform this reality: the wealth gap in the United States is racialized and people tend to have friend groups who are largely like them.

Some of the women in these networks took up our "founding DNA" finding as a challenge and I love that. Do it and I'll try to help you! But just like many women's funds and foundations were begun a generation or two ago because those women found the philanthropic vehicles set up by their grandfathers, fathers, uncles, and brothers to be inadequate, some folks of color are finding they'd like a philanthropic home of their own, too.

JACK IS REACHING across the aisle, to borrow a political expression, because he wants to feel uncomfortable on purpose in order to grow. Jack grew up in Raleigh, North Carolina, to parents who were both educators. One next-door neighbor showed young Jack the tattoo that marked him a survivor of the Holocaust in Nazi Germany, and another taught him how to cook hamburgers on bunched-up balls of newspaper because it's cheaper than charcoal. He went to public schools, got an ROTC scholarship to attend college, and served in the U.S. Air Force. With his electrical engineering degree, Jack started out doing information technology at big, brand-name companies, then moved into consulting and investing, got an MBA, worked in two start-ups, had two "exits," one of which was a unicorn (which means the start-up had a value of $1 billion or more when it was acquired or went public), and now lives in an affluent suburb of a large U.S. city.

Jack is white, in his midfifties, married, and an involved dad with three kids. Politically, he says of himself, "I don't consider myself conservative, although people in [his very liberal town] might. I am very fiscally conservative, strong on national defense, small on government, socially moderate, and tolerant. I wouldn't call myself socially liberal. I would call myself in the 'live and let live' camp."

Jack grew up a devout Lutheran; "I was swaddled in the faith," as he puts it. When we met, he was frustrated with the homogeneity of his faith community in his town. "Not only was it homogenous in terms of political views, it was an ocean of old white people. It wasn't helping me grow in the faith. I wasn't getting anything to help me understand the world better, to expand my worldview." He told me that of all the many communities he is part of, he realized it was his faith community, oriented around meaning, values, and finding higher purpose, that ought to be expansive.

So he switched churches. He found a congregation in the town next door that is more diverse along age, race and ethnicity, nationality, and especially along socioeconomic lines. The congregation is very welcoming of LGBTQ+ people. The senior minister is a forty-year-old Korean American mother of two. Jack says of her, "As a person and a minister, she is openly questioning all manner of things. She is super thoughtful and provocative, almost shocking at times. This is quite helpful, since I recently realized that while I've studied many things in life, including a graduate degree in business, I've never, ever questioned my faith at even a first-grade level. This community is what I was looking for in diversity of viewpoints and culture, which is perfect for where I'm at in life."

Jack is relishing the intellectual and faith tussle that he's found at his new church. He put himself—on purpose—into a community in which he is a minority. When I brought that to his attention, he said, "Not only did I put myself into that position, I'm thriving!" Jack is working closely with the senior minister to develop the church's mission, vision, and strategy, a fun re-exercising of his consulting chops, and he also serves on what functions as the lay board of directors.

In ways small and large, Jack is moving from a Me position to a We position. Jack is challenging himself to find belonging with people who are not like him. He's also having a ball. He made an intentional decision to find a more expansive faith community, and in doing so, ended up expanding himself by digging in.

GIVING PROJECTS ARE another model of collective giving, but unlike most giving circles, they are facilitated and staffed by social justice public foundations. Giving Projects purposefully build bridges across differences by putting together cohorts of fifteen to twenty everyday people, intentionally diverse across race, class, and other identities. Over a six-month period, participants make a personally meaningful gift, raise money through one-on-one grassroots fundraising within their communities, learn about local social justice movements, and democratically make grants to support local constituent-led community organizing. Since 2010, Giving Projects have trained thousands of participants as donor organizers and moved over $20 million to grassroots community organizing, donated from over 22,000 donors. Because they are professionally facilitated, Giving Projects are expensive to run, but they're transformative for the participants.

Tracy Gagnon participated in a Giving Project at Social Justice Fund Northwest and now works for the national network of funds using this model. She grew up in Las Vegas with a Chinese mother and a white father, both having worked in casinos. She joined a Giving Project after the 2016 presidential election. She told me, "For me, it was a profound opportunity to get grounded during a politically unstable time. I was drawn to it because it was designed to be intentionally diverse with a clear purpose: to collectively move money to local community organizing. When everything felt so big and out of my control, this was a space where I felt like I could actually do something. And we did. I was so moved by what our small cohort did together in six months.

We were held through a collective journey of personal and historical discovery, while getting practical skills to bring our communities along with us. When, at the time, we were told that our goal would be to move $100,000 together, I thought it was impossible, but nothing is impossible when a group of people are committed to a shared purpose. We exceeded our goal and we were able to fund seven organizations at $20,000 each."

About the group conversations around race, class, families, and money, Tracy said, "I was terrified of fundraising; I was that girl who dropped out of Girl Scouts because I didn't want to sell cookies … It was very uncomfortable. But I ended up making the biggest gift I'd ever made, and that was true for many in my cohort. Since then, I've given more and larger amounts. I have gotten creative about how to raise money for different causes, like a garage sale and a backyard movie screening on reproductive justice."

Most Giving Projects raise a minimum of $100,000. Because the groups are so diverse along class and financial capacity, there's a big range in what people give. A personally meaningful gift for one participant might be $5, and for another, $50,000, and there is often meaning beyond the dollar amount. One working class Native Hawaiian participant in Hawai'i People's Fund's 2021 Giving Project gave a meaningful gift of $128 to represent the years of U.S. occupation.

Sian Miranda Singh ÓFaoláin is a codirector of the national Giving Project Network. Sian identifies as Black, and of Caribbean and Irish heritage. When she was considering the amount of her meaningful gift in a Giving Project focused on Black-led organizing, she thought, "Okay, what's the amount I can easily drop for a family member who needs it? I'll double that amount for this. This is an amount I can do with a little planning over a few months." Sian describes Giving Projects as small utopias.

Giving Projects create "these beautiful, cross-race, cross-class, well-facilitated spaces; spaces made with care, thought, and deep intention. It shows people what is possible, and the kind of society we want, where we organize resources to meet collective needs. We can see what is possible when everyone gets to share their struggles. We're here for a purpose. We're building relationships and pushing toward a better world."

As Karen Orrick, who spent five years co-facilitating Giving Projects at Bread & Roses Community Fund in Philadelphia, put it, "In Giving Projects, we're in the business of giving people hope."

MARIO LUGAY, one of my dear friends in the collective giving movement, speaks eloquently about political homes as places where we can find other people who want to engage, grapple, and make community, and, ultimately, make change in the world around us. He describes a typical journey: Someone starts off with some unsustainable feeling—like sadness, concern, or guilt—about something happening in their community. She looks for people who have that same feeling, and together, they have experiences that counter those sad ones, like joy or laughter or bonhomie. Bolstered by this community, she is able to take action to address the underlying causes of the feelings that brought them together in the first place. As Mario describes it, civic engagement arises in the pairing of the "bad" feelings with the "good" ones. When bad things happen in the world, we want to turn to our communities to make sense of it, to collectively work through what it might mean, and finally and most crucially, to consider what we might do to address it together. These networks of concerned friends and neighbors constitute political homes, places where we can talk about what's troubling us and then actually do something about it, together.

Mario experienced his first political home at the Coalition Against Anti-Asian Violence in New York City in the 1990s. According to the 2020 census, Asian Americans are about 7.2 percent of the U.S. population today, yet receive less than one half of 1 percent of all philanthropic dollars. In New York City, Asian Americans represent 15.6 percent of the population and are the racial/ethnic group with the highest rates of poverty, with one in five Asians in the city being classified as poor. Yet Asian American led and serving organizations receive only 4.66 percent of the city council's discretionary dollars.[6] The representational disparity in funding is inimical to fairness and need.

Asian Americans can be invisible as a racial minority. When I started the AWGC, I wanted us to be housed at the New York Women's Foundation, on whose board I served. They declined because we weren't rich enough and, I think, because they didn't consider us enough of a minority in a binary world that is black and white. While it did hurt my heart that the NYWF couldn't find or imagine a room for us in their house, it remains an important philanthropic and political home for me personally. So much so that I've included it as a charitable beneficiary in my will.

The AWGC endeavors to be an antiracist project because we are building community and solidarity within our sisterhood, *and* we are actively aligning ourselves in solidarity with other marginalized communities. We assert that we belong in philanthropic spaces. We assert, loudly, proudly, and with joy, this idea that "I see you, and you see me" across many shades of difference. Listening, inviting, witnessing, and accompanying are the building blocks of building belonging. We are creating a political home together.

. . .

GIVING CIRCLES, like most things, benefit from tending. But when we're talking about a collective, the idea of leader can seem like an oxymoron. When I think about the giving circles I know, often the best leaders are the ones whose styles I might describe as not too leaderful—someone who is less pulpit and more pew, less boss and more collaborator, more coach and less star player. And also, dare I say it, someone who sparks some joy?

A leader who is more We than Me.

One way to be more We than Me is to keep the larger vision at the fore. Reverend Dr. Starsky Wilson is the president and CEO of the Children's Defense Fund, which was founded by the legendary educator, lawyer, children's advocate, and civil rights leader Marian Wright Edelman. The Children's Defense Fund has an expansive mission to ensure a level playing field for all children. They educate, advocate, raise awareness, analyze data, publish research, share best practices, advocate for legislation, and push for policies that benefit the most vulnerable children. In other words, they do *a lot*.

I've been fortunate to meet Rev. Starsky on a few occasions, and I heard him speak at a conference in 2023. He asked us to think of a child who is dear to us. Put that child in your mind, he told us. (He's a kind, commanding, compelling reverend, so one tends to do just as one is told . . .) See her in your mind's eye, hear her giggle, smell the smells of what she's been snacking on, feel her big run-jump hug. Rather than list all the many things the Children's Defense Fund does, Rev. Starsky was able to distill his vision into one expansive, beautiful image: "Now picture that child dancing. Freedom is when happy, well, and whole children sing and dance."[7]

Rev. Starsky encapsulates his expansive vision into one beautiful sentence, and his vision cannot help but bring a warm smile into your heart. His is a beautiful image you can literally see, feel, and touch. It's way more memorable than the dozens of activities the organization lists on its website.

Keeping everyone's eyeballs on the higher vision at least some of the time is a really important part of exercising our civic engagement muscles. Remembering that we share some most important dreams, values, and purpose helps us weather the disagreements and conflicts that will inevitably arise. My friend Daniel Lee, former head of the Levi Strauss Foundation, calls this skill "finding the Buddha in the room." The more we can practice this together, the better equipped we will be to participate civically.

When I think about navigating disagreements and holding the larger vision, the word that comes to mind for me, again, is *grace*. My friend Joy Webb, giving circle emissary and founder of Circle of Joy in Atlanta, says, "It's a giving circle, but it's a forgiving circle." Vision and commitment go a long way, but it's easiest to access grace when there is friendship, regard, community, and relationships.

Giving circles offer the ideal conditions to flex and strengthen the interpersonal dynamics that are so key to collective action, whether that's working with neighbors across the street or across the aisle.

FANDOMS, OR ONLINE FAN COMMUNITIES, are fascinating to me. They're like a viral form of belonging, community building that is catching. They're super grassroots, guerrilla organizing. I include them here because there is so much potential to touch, reach, and activate millions of people across pop culture and fandoms.

Crystal Thompkins is a Gen-Xer who calls North Carolina home. She worked for years at a big bank and has recently joined a start-up financial advisory firm. She's a financial advisor who knows the intricate ins and outs of estate planning. She's also a super fan. As we're talking on Zoom, I can see behind her album cover magnets, a row of actual albums, and a Prophecy Girl figurine from the world of *Buffy the Vampire Slayer*.

Crystal told me recently, "I went straight from fan to super fan, or *stan* as in the Eminem song." She's been to a dozen Depeche Mode concerts around the country. But it was Buffy that introduced Crystal to fandoms. Buffy was Crystal's first experience interacting with an online fan community. "You watch a show, then you immediately go online and find thousands of people ready to talk about that experience and your feelings around it. The internet then was different—you could longform it, share long narratives publicly. Now it's bits and pieces with lots of ads. Then, it was LiveJournal or Tumblr or Myspace, and you could type till you got tired. And people would read, respond, do the same! It was a dialogue, truly. Buffy tackled so many things, like losing a parent, being new and finding friends, falling in love for the first time, being a girl, being an oldest girl. I felt like I was part of something, with a bunch of other people. After a while, you feel like, 'Okay, I know these people.'"

To the great consternation of her husband, Crystal decided to meet her internet stranger friends in real life. She drove to DC by herself to meet up with fifteen other stranger friends from the *Buffy* fandom. They stayed at one woman's house for three days, watched *Buffy*, and talked about it. Later, Crystal joined seventy-five *Buffy* fans at RedNeck.com in Nashville. She's flying to California next week for work and will meet up with two women with whom she's been friends for twenty-five years via fandoms. These three are learning Korean, have a passing knowledge of *hangul* (the Korean alphabet), and are planning a trip to Korea next year.

Crystal first got into BTS, the worldwide-phenom K-Pop band, for their music. Then she learned that BTS had donated $1 million to Black Lives Matter, which was promptly matched by thirty-five thousand of their fans from all over the world, who raised an additional $1 million in twenty-four hours in small-dollar donations.[8]

BTS fans are called the ARMY, which is an acronym for Adorable Representative M.C. for Youth. They are not formally organized, they're massively online, and together, they're incredible. The mostly teenage members of the ARMY punked the Trump campaign, reserving thousands of tickets for a rally in Tulsa, Oklahoma, that they never intended to attend. Trump's campaign manager bragged that a million tickets had been sold, then the massive arena ended up being embarrassingly empty.[9] They've raised over $1 million for charitable efforts around the world, including $11,146 (from 437 donors in over fifty countries) for comprehensive cleft palate surgery and care; $2,268 (from 168 donors) for pets for the elderly; and $2,370 (from 176 donors in over forty countries) for a center for children with disabilities in Haiti.[10]

Unlike most other musician-led fundraising efforts, BTS fans are self-organized into a group, ONE IN AN ARMY, that hosts fundraising events for causes and also tracks the global causes that ARMYs are participating in around the world. The Philippine ARMY is currently raising money for farmers. Crystal says, "It's all well organized, by fans. It's nimble and really quick in response times. The tracking is amazing. I've seen ARMYs mobilize super quick within distinct, separate, and representative sectors. There are ARMY gardeners, hospital workers, lawyers, people who work at NASA. The connectivity is amazing and it is truly global."

Crystal is moderating an ARMY forum now that raises money for ARMYs that don't have access to albums, like for fans in India, Pakistan, and Bangladesh. She and her coleader, also named Crystal, raise money to get them access to BTS's music. The other Crystal is nineteen, second-generation Asian American, and writing a thesis on the activation and power of online fandoms. She has a podcast and is leading activist initiatives around Palestine and other causes. They've never met in real life. They communicate mostly via an app called Discord, which is kind of like Slack. The Crystal I know has the fandom name True Crystal. And she says, "Hey, I'm flying my fandom flag loud and proud! We love BTS. That's where it started. They've inspired us to love ourselves, be good people, and do good things to help other people. Purple is our color, the color of the ARMY. If we could capture that spirit across other areas, the possibilities are literally endless."

Projects that build belonging can be as small as one giving circle or as large as a fandom. I think a big part of building belonging is creating spaces where people feel seen: I see you and you see me. I wrote the *Portrait* report so donors of color would feel seen in the philanthropic literature. Building belonging is also the feeling of home. That feeling of home is hard to describe, but you know it when you feel it. Andine feels it with the Asian Women Giving Circle, and so do I. Feeling a part of something makes you care for it more. And if you're part of that thing with other people, that feeling of comradery and interconnectedness makes you care for it even more. Moving from a Me to a We builds that virtuous cycle of care, mutuality, interdependence, and responsibility. And when the object of that mutual, shared care is a community, neighborhood, fandom, or giving circle, there is tremendous power in the group to effect change together.

Exercising Our Civic Engagement Muscles by Doing It Together

Recall from earlier chapters that we Americans are polarized and increasingly uncivil. We're lonely and it's literally killing us. We long to belong and crave community. We need each other but we don't know how to do it, with whom, or where. Big Phil, billionaire-led, "I alone can fix it" philanthropy cannot fix it. But giving circles maybe can, or at the very least, they're a great way to try. Giving circles are vehicles to build belonging in purposeful and intentional communities. They're a natural container for organizing regular people into engaged groups of citizens who want to do things like add traffic bumps on a busy street, deal with the rats partying in the garbage (like on my block), raise awareness about a piece of state legislation that cuts money to schools, or mobilize for clean air, good jobs, and control over our own bodies. These are actions that describe civic engagement, and our democratic system relies on citizens who care enough to get civically engaged.

Are you already part of a book group, adult sports team, exercise or walking or parenting group? Do you talk about the state of things, goings-on in your community, social issues, or upcoming elections? That's civic engagement.

And if ever there was a time when we need to exercise our civic engagement muscles, it is now.

LISA GOLDENBERG CORN is that mom who routinely bailed me out. Her two kids are the same ages as two of my kids, and thank god for Lisa because she always knew when the parent-teacher signups were, what date the field trip was, and when the kids needed to show up in some costume or with some baked good offering.

There are two concepts in Lisa's faith that have been a throughline for her civic engagement. The first is *tikkun olam*, which means "repair of the world." Lisa tells me that this means Jews are called upon to make the world more peaceful, just, tolerant, and equal through acts of charity, kindness, and political action. For Lisa, being raised in the Jewish tradition conditioned her to think of others in this way: "working to repair the world, making things better." The second aspect of Lisa's faith that guides her is *tzedakah*, which is helping others, classically exemplified by saving a portion of the harvest for poorer people. "There's always someone who is less fortunate than you, or who may not have a voice," she explained. "You've got to do what you can, to use your privilege as we'd say now, to do what you can."

Lisa didn't really see herself as an organizer until after the 2016 election, when, like so many people, she found herself reaching for ways to push back against what she saw as the rising tides of injustice. In early 2017, one of her friends stumbled on some Get Out the Vote (GOTV) postcard writing groups and materials. They organized a group of friends, and every week, twenty or so women met at a Le Pain Quotidien in downtown Manhattan near their kids' schools. They wrote GOTV cards and went together to weekly actions. They organized the writing and the stamp buying. "It felt so good to have a place where we could learn together and do something. And have a place where it was okay to talk about our fears, worries, hopes, politics."

These moms built community with each other via their shared upset and their shared desire to do something about it. And once they got together, they found they wanted to do more. What could this group of women do on top of writing, calling, knitting pussy hats, marching, and protesting?

They could add money.

I connected Lisa's group with Melissa Walker, a Brooklynite, author, and mom. Melissa had started a giving circle with her fellow kid-lit authors, writers, agents, and booksellers focused on building power in state legislatures, and she was building a national network of giving circles focused on doing the same. Lisa remembers that first meeting with Melissa. "Melissa got us very excited. But we were all like 'no way.' Are you kidding me? Asking people for money? I hate talking about money. No way can we ask people for money. We cannot raise $150,000. No way. Plus, we didn't really understand the importance of state legislatures then, like I didn't even know who my state representative was!"

Lisa and the others were familiar with the idea of fundraising for their kids' schools and for their churches and synagogues. But like many of us, they were petrified to talk about money with their friends, and even worse, to ask for donations! They decided to go on fundraising "asks" in pairs. Lisa said that on her first foray, she could barely stammer out the words. Their first big donation was $5,000, followed soon after by a couple who gave $10,000. "Melissa taught us to make yourself say a bigger number. Wait for that uncomfortable silence. But that uncomfortable silence was *so* uncomfortable for us!"

This group of uncomfortable women has gone on to raise over $1 million in five years.

Lisa's group is now part of a national network of giving circles that focuses on building power in state legislatures. State legislatures are responsible for almost every issue that directly affects our lives, like quality public education, clean water, more affordable housing, public safety, transportation, access to healthcare and reproductive services including abortion, accessible and affordable childcare, and the freedom to vote. The States Project engages thousands of citizens in dozens of giving circles, all laser focused on state legislative bodies and state races, because it is in states that we can build governing majorities that will improve the lives of working people and families.

Lisa's circle voted to put its money into Michigan for three years before the party they supported gained a governing majority. Until the 2022 midterms, Michigan hadn't had a Democrat "trifecta" (when all three branches, the Michigan House, Senate, and governorship, are the same party) since 1984. In its first one hundred days of controlling the state government, the Democrats boosted union workers, expanded protections for LGBTQ+ people, officially repealed the state's 1931 abortion ban, repealed its retirement tax, introduced safe storage laws for guns, and expanded the state's earned income tax credit—all wins for the state's working families.[1]

The giving circle of New York City moms was a big part of funding those wins. What started as a group of moms concerned about local issues eventually transformed into a powerful political collective, joining with other collectives to influence national politics. Lisa and her circle mates feel like they played a part in those wins for working families in a state a thousand miles away. They are so pumped to be more engaged citizens, adding money to the power of their voice and convictions.

What's next for Lisa and her group? Lisa says, "My mission is to not stop because there's no off-year or downtime. Also to stay steady because people do come back. If my hair's on fire about something, I'll call and organize, and together we'll get through it." Lisa has connected her faith and cultural values of *tikkun olam* and *tzedakah* with civic engagement and political action. Even though many in her group are not Jewish, she has built community around her values and faith tradition. She is engaged in repairing her world in ways both micro and macro: weekly breakfasts with engaged neighbors who are, together, trying to fortify our democracy as best they can.

Melissa Walker runs the national giving circle project that includes Lisa's group. Mario Lugay introduced us when Melissa was thinking about turning her own giving circle into a national network of them. Melissa is the author of eight young adult (YA) novels including the Violet on the Runway series and *Small Town Sinners.*[2] She grew up in Chapel Hill, North Carolina, and told me that until recently, she had been fairly unpolitical. Like the Le Pain Quotidien moms, she'd become angry, scared, and energized after the 2016 election. After hearing State Senator Daniel Squadron speak at a holiday party, she realized that focusing on state legislatures, and doing it collectively, could bring true impact, because Daniel told them it was often cheaper to change the balance of power in a state chamber than it was to win a single competitive congressional seat. Melissa mobilized her kid-lit community of authors, agents, booksellers, and librarians to pool their dollars politically. They ended up moving $250,000 their first year, then $800,000, then $1.3 million to state legislative elections with the aim of flipping their state legislative bodies from red to blue. She told me that after the 2016 election, she felt like "there was a house on fire next door, and I had to grab a hose." Instead of losing herself in frustration, she found other people who were sad, frustrated, and felt helpless and angry. She activated her community, starting with the few people she knew who had recently sold their books to TV and Hollywood. Once her circle was moving, she wanted others to organize this way. So she teamed up with Daniel Squadron, who had started The States Project in 2017, very soon after Melissa heard him speak. Together, they thought, "Hey, we should do this around the country! And PACs (political action committees) are actually really complicated, so let's figure out a way to make it easier for the groups who want to do what we did." Today, Melissa runs The States Project's Giving Circle program, a national network of hundreds of giving circles around the country mobilizing tens of thousands of people to move their values via their money toward creating new governing power in state legislatures.[3]

Motivated by her personal upset, Melissa tapped into her community to create a giving circle, and now, spurred by the collective power of We, into growing a national movement. Melissa took what she'd done with her community of writers, agents, and booksellers and multiplied it by a thousand. My group of mom friends has grown into a leading giving circle within The States Project's network, which was begun in 2017 by Daniel Squadron, a former New York State senator. In the 2022 midterm election cycle, the group moved $60 million into state legislative efforts. As Melissa eloquently says, "Everything you care about is decided in states. Good jobs. Quality public education. Clean air and water. Rights to reproductive health. Lowering costs for working families. All of this gets decided in state legislatures, not in Washington, DC." Furthermore, state legislative races are relatively inexpensive to run. It's often cheaper to change the balance of power in a state chamber than it is to win a single, competitive congressional seat.[4] And while Melissa could not have afforded to fund a legislative campaign by herself, she did learn to mobilize her network of friends, colleagues, and neighbors to collectively raise a meaningful amount of money to make real change on the state level.

Melissa added, "Doing these political giving circles is the most powerful thing I've ever done, and the most inspiring thing I've ever worked on. I see the change that's happening, I see other people learning how to make that change. If people learn how to organize in a giving circle context, to bring attention and resources to the things they care about, then they walk through the world with more power. And if we all have that skill, we'd all be able to work through the world, with our values on display, and bring other people with us. And I find this to be so therapeutic in this moment when things don't feel so stable."[5]

As the States Project says on its website, "When you elect people who are focused on improving peoples' lives, that's when policies change." In 2018, Melissa worked with two giving circles who concentrated their efforts on trying to change the balance of power in the Maine state senate. It worked. And in August the next year, Democratic lawmakers who comprised a new majority in the state raised teacher pay by $40,000, expanded environmental protections and healthcare for women, and reduced the cost of prescription drugs. The price tag for flipping the state legislature in Maine in 2018? $150,000. Two giving circles were able to raise the money to make a real change in the lives of Maine's citizens.

The moms group at Le Pain Quotidien is one of hundreds of States Projects giving circles. They are formally known as the Downtown Nasty Women Social Group and they've moved over $150,000 in each of the past three election cycles. In 2023, they passed the $1 million mark of money moved to elect candidates in state legislatures. Via their involvement in the States Project network, these women are more educated, more organized, more energized, and more committed than ever to working to see that local governments serve all our actual real-life needs. Being part of a giving circle has made these women better citizens. And our democracy works better when its citizens are informed, engaged, and active.

Giving circles are one way to engage with the many large, complex social problems that need many, many solutions. They perfectly marry the personal and the political. They bring together the philanthropic impulse and the civic impulse and tie both to the demand that we work hard, together, to insist that our governments serve us, the people.

Giving Circles like these help move us from the Me to the We to the Big We.

And this kind of collective action is just not possible through elite, Big Phil philanthropy. Big Phil could help grow collective action by funding the giving circle movement. It could throw its weight behind the local work done by giving circles by matching their dollars.

Melissa's story started with her, but it didn't remain with her. It *started* as an individual, but it didn't *remain* with an individual. First, she found ten people who shared her concerns, and today, that group numbers in the thousands. Instead of a billionaire-led, top-down solution that often went awry, this was a community-led solution that is really working. The impulse to get personally involved in issues that are important to us and make change isn't wrong, but the method and narrative around it needs to go beyond the lone individual and his means or desires. Less Me, more We.

Melissa created something that goes way beyond traditional philanthropy, too. She is using every vehicle available to her while staying within the rules of the law. That means cash dollars, 501(c)(3) dollars, and 501(c)(4) and PAC (political action) dollars as well as, of course, all her other *T*'s. Lisa's group uses all their Five *T*'s, too: they make phone calls, volunteer their time, march at rallies, influence other circles and friends to give, leverage their networks to their case, and of course, give and raise a lot of money, too.

The States Project giving circle network is growing both in terms of people engaged and dollars moved, and they're all involved in the political process in the United States. They're a great example of individuals coming together to form groups that then join a larger network to build a more engaged citizenry who cares about making our communities better for all. All these individuals have moved from Me to We to Big We and they're going strong.

Giving circles can be, for many, our new churches, our college dorms, our town squares. We can intentionally gather friends, coworkers, and neighbors around common values, causes, even shared dreams. In this way, giving circles can fill a gap in our increasingly atomized society. I don't go to church or a place of worship. I don't go to college and no longer live in a dorm. I don't belong to a sorority or civic club or social club where I might pop in and find friends. Like many of my contemporaries, I'm super busy with work, kids, partner, elderly parents. As a result of all this, I don't have the time or a place to go to talk about important things. My giving circle has become that place. I'm so thankful for my giving circle sisters and the ways we're creating a community within the larger community of New York City around shared values and shared purpose. But we don't stop there; we move money and actions together, too.

It is in the wrangling, the going back and forth, the negotiating, arguing, and sometimes reaching consensus that we exercise our civic engagement muscles. We have to talk about our shared values even when it's hard. We have to talk about what we want to see happen in our communities, and this can be hard, too. There's a big argument right now about a municipal jail going up in Chinatown. Reasonable people disagree, but some pretty dire compromises were made on the part of a large community-based organization in the neighborhood. Talking about this local issue with the circle sisters is a civic engagement exercise, too. We might hone an argument pro or con, almost in preparation for a larger conversation with others later. We decide together where to give our Five T's, and that is another aspect of being engaged in the civic life of our city. We might decide *not* to do an action as a group, but then some of us might do so as an individual or with another group—again, a strategy for how to get more engaged in the life of our neighborhood, community, and city. Even thinking about the life of our town and city, even dreaming about what might be—is such an important part of being civically engaged.

It is exhilarating to do all this with a group of girlfriends. I encourage you to wade in and try.

By building community, Melissa was able to create something that is more than the sum of its parts. By a lot. I've been an executive director, a development director, and a board member for various nonprofits, and I know from experience that the donors with the most impact are the ones who can mobilize others to join the cause. I've seen again and again how ten donors who give $100 each are more valuable than one donor who gives $1,000. Why? Because if even a fraction of those donors donates again, or contributes to the work in some other way, the organization has outstripped the contributions of the single $1,000 donor. Even more importantly, each of the ten $100 donors is connected to multiple and varied networks and might also bring in a friend or friends of their own. Finally, each of those ten donors brings their different life experience and perspective to the organization's work—and that diversity of experiences is critical for a healthy organizational ecosystem. Don't get me wrong—the one donor who gives the big gift is valuable to any nonprofit. But from the organizational standpoint, the home run is that big donor who brings along her friends. The ability to multiply and amplify is a giving circle's superpower.

Giving circles can be incredibly effective in creating awareness, marshaling volunteers, and raising funds, but perhaps equally important is the way that they can also lay the groundwork for systemic change. By systemic change, I mean actions that get to the underlying policies, practices, social norms, and power dynamics in which we all work and live—like tax policy, who represents us as elected officials, and even the narratives that we absorb via small and large screens. We saw this with Sara and Lyord earlier. Sara has transformed her Mexican, Catholic heritage into an international infrastructure organization that brings thousands of individuals into the giving circle movement, moving millions of dollars mostly toward small, local grassroots organizations. Lisa and Melissa use their giving circle experiences to make systemic change by focusing time, attention, and resources on state legislative bodies. The Asian Women Giving Circle focuses its efforts on changing the narrative of Asian American women and gender expansive folks as storytellers, donors, creators, doers, and activists. Lyord's giving circle was a springboard to local elected office, and he's now taking his giving circle experience toward mobilizing more Black wealth in his area. He's tackling the racial wealth gap and its historic, systemic roots in his town. It's almost a kind of magic—the ability of a collective, animated by shared values and purpose, to multiply its power, while moving money, building community, and making social change.

There's a multiplier effect when you engage more than one. If we look at the individual power we each hold—in our families, jobs, socioeconomic status, education, networks, and so on—it can be substantial. Put a few of us into a living room, organize a conversation, and the power of that room multiplies to become something far bigger than any individual hero can accomplish alone.

In your mind's eye, picture an America where millions of people are engaged in thousands of groups, each composed of citizens who care about their towns and neighborhoods. They meet, share food and conversation, and talk about the values and issues that are important to them. They identify common ones, then apply those values to actions that make their neighborhoods and cities more fair, more representative, and better for more of their fellow citizens to live in. Imagine that "we can do this" spirit applied to electing a government that represents more of us.

These civic groups, these groups of citizens, these giving circles, are built upon relationships in which there is community and growing trust, and in which individuals know each other. We are each other's regulars. We know about each other's work, families, kids, schools, hobbies. We might vote for different political parties, but we come together about the neighborhood playground, public schools, and clean water. Relationships and community are the preconditions upon which consensus, dissent, and disagreement can occur. Though we differ and are different, we have issues we care about in common—and it is around that civic square that we can come together around common purpose to do good things for our communities.

If we tweak that American "can do" spirit from "I alone can do this" to "we can do this together!" our voices ring truer and are exponentially more powerful. If we can move from Me to We to a Big We, we are greater than the sum of our parts. We can switch from billionaire-focused to people-powered, and that is a gamechanger.

AS WE REIMAGINE building a more people-powered form of philanthropy, let's change the setting. If Big Phil presides from a corporate boardroom, giving circles reside in living rooms and kitchen tables.

Kitchen tables have been the locus of a lot of powerful organizing, especially for those of us who have been excluded historically from country club golf courses and corporate boardrooms. Kitchen tables are where real talk happens and decisions get made. They're multipurpose, and mine, as yours probably does, too, morphs from breakfast to homework to dinner to dumpling making to holiday gatherings to bedtime tea. At our place, we've hosted giving circle, block association, and committee meetings around the table and written thousands of postcards for candidates and causes, usually with lots of good food and bring-your-own-beverages.

The work of social change can feel, sometimes, like sanctimonious drudgery. Let's imagine it, instead, as something that can happen, in community, with laughter, food, and friends, around a well-used table. If you've got people sitting around your table, you're building relationship and connection with them. You've invited them in, or you've been invited in. You are listening, sharing, tussling, accompanying.

Your kitchen table can be the site of some incredible organizing, too. Start table-size, then add a leaf or two to add folks slightly beyond your usual friend group. Start small in order to dream big.

10

The Secret Sauce

It was a hot, sticky, late summer day. We were about forty women, and a few good men, most of us sunkissed and sweaty, all of us smiling. We gathered in the garden of the Mertz Gilmore Foundation near Irving Place in downtown Manhattan to welcome new grantee partners to the Asian Women Giving Circle family. The Garden Party is my favorite of our annual events. After an hour or so of mingling and noshing, we came together as one big group. One by one, we tossed each other a big ball of bright pink yarn. As each person caught the ball, she shared one thing she appreciated about this community. Among the responses: "The sisterhood ... the funding! ... that we're all in this together ... all of you for convening us ... the solidarity ... the work that you do ... the art and social change you make ... that you exist for us, with us ... YOU, ALL OF US, our community." They wrapped the yarn around their wrists then tossed the ball to someone else. By the end, everyone had shared a thought, and we were all connected by the same ball of bright pink yarn.

Picture all forty of us in that garden, tied together by one bright pink string, a messy web, an interwoven cosmos, a tangled tapestry, each and all, nothing and everything.

The final step in this activity is cutting the string. Each participant is left with enough string around their wrist to make a bracelet. You need help from another to cut the yarn and to tie a good knot. I said to the group as our goodbye that late summer night, "Thank you for celebrating our community together with us this evening. Wear this string bracelet. Every time you look at it, remember how you are feeling right now and the words you heard. Tell your friends about it. Remember this feeling of being in this work together. Remember each other. When the string falls off, it falls off. But we'll always remember this evening and what we're building together."

I've been in this collective giving space for so long, I often get asked, what's the secret sauce? How have you kept this thing going with such energy, passion, and good humor? And truthfully, the longer I do this, the more that answer gets distilled. The secret sauce is two parts building belonging and one part keeping it fun, at least some of the time.

Joy and belonging are the throughlines, the constants, the glue that keeps us going for the long haul.

Even with something that seems as dry as a neighborhood block association, there can be a colorful cast of personalities, muddling along with humor, a sense of purpose, and shared goals, for the good of the group.

My neighborhood block association is obsessed with rats and trees. In my opinion, I live on one of the most beautiful blocks in Brooklyn. I love my block and my neighborhood. When we first stumbled across this block, we met our future neighbor Heidi who lived next to Anne (who soon moved, sadly), who lives next to Mary—and all their kids were scampering up and down the block like rug rats. Peter and I could just *see* our kids joining that mad, dirty, chattering pack. Our fates were sealed.

Eighteen years later, our kids have grown up here. We're both members of the block association and Peter is the newly elected, volun-told president. Our neighbor Christel hilariously intones, "Well hello, Mr. President," when they pass on the street. Our neighbor Rae has lived in the house across the street since the 1970s. She worked for many years in city government and knows how to get things done. She has been the Rat Czar and the Tree Queen of the block for many years.

During COVID, the rat population in New York City soared. It's gross. The rats are big and bold. One literally ran over my foot the other night while I was walking our dog, Stu. You can see big plastic trash bags on the sidewalk that are bumping and wriggling from the rat activity inside.

Rae, bless her, focuses on rats for the benefit of all of us. She educates us and tells us what to do. The block commissioned a rat study, and one terrifying day, we all received a two-hundred-page PDF that detailed every single lot's rat exposure and responsibility. Rae testifies about the rats at the city council on behalf of our block. Her emails say things like "Join me for Rat Academy," and "They're still among us. Put a lid on your trash," and "Before the hearing started, Rocco spoke with the director of Rodent Mitigation (a.k.a. Rat Czar), Kathy Corradi. He was impressed that she remembered him from a S.C.R.A.M. 'rat walk' on Sterling Place many months ago . . ." Obviously everyone needs a neighbor like Rae.

Trees are another concern. We have these beautiful, stately London plane trees that line our entire block. Unfortunately, sometimes branches fall and damage cars or even houses but, thank goodness, no humans yet. They require regular maintenance. Our block tries to notice when a branch looks rotten. Paul, married to Christel next door, spearheaded a fundraising effort to plant new trees in empty tree spots. Peter, another neighbor, used to head up a similar effort to plant daffodils in the tree pits.

On New Year's Day 2024, another neighbor sent around this sweet email to the block LISTSERV: "Happy New Year, everyone! Here's hoping for less rats, more trees, and peace and justice for all in 2024. Grateful to know you and be in this community."

Like I said, I love my block.

It's not always roses, though. We've had disagreements over the noise produced by nearby bars, alternate side of the street parking, speed bumps or not, location of CitiBike parking spots, support or non-support of nearby new developments, and so on. Like many New York City neighborhoods, our block ranges from "old timers" who are retired city government employees and public-school teachers to newer comers who are lawyers, bankers, or have some family money, who are just wealthier.

The block association has been at times very active (like block parties every summer, regular representation at city council meetings, huddles with other block associations) and other times, moribund. We're coming out of moribund and hopefully moving into a slightly more active phase. The older residents are asking the newer ones to step up, and luckily, they're still around to advise.

Block associations like mine are another forum for civic engagement.

Like the community the AWGC has built, tied together by pink yarn at that garden party a few years ago, the denizens of my block belong to one another. In fact, we neighbors are literally stuck together because our homes are all connected; like a typical brownstone neighborhood we share party walls with the homes adjacent. But we've taken some extra steps because we care about the block. We care about rats, trees, our neighborhood, and our city. We care enough to put a little time, talent, treasure, testimony, and ties into improving and helping those things. We've organized ourselves into a group of citizens who take actions together to improve our community. We step up and step back as we are able and have time. We gather around each other's kitchen tables to break bread, share wine, gossip a little, and help each other out and improve our neighborhood. With time, we've grown to care for each other, too.

As important as it is to keep our eyes fixed on our shared vision for change, it's also important to occasionally take our feet off the gas—and focus less on the what and more on the how. How are we spending time together? Are we prioritizing laughter, getting to know one another better, and community building? The AWGC tries not to meet in boardrooms; a member's living room or a big table at a favorite restaurant feels less like a chore. If we do have to congregate under fluorescent lighting, anyone who can make it goes out for a drink or dinner afterward. We work hard, but we also add outings that have no agenda other than seeing some interesting cultural happening and being with each other. We don't consider this a waste of time because we agree that when giving is fun, it's stickier.

In fact, we take enjoying our time together so seriously that the Asian Women Giving Circle has a steering committee role that is the "cruise director." Her role is to organize our social events—sometimes just the sisters of the AWGC, sometimes for our larger community. Recently, our outings have included a wine tasting at Rooftop Reds in the Brooklyn Navy Yard, a trip to see the cherry blossoms at the Brooklyn Botanical Garden, a movie outing during the Asian American Film Festival, a picnic at Shakespeare in the Park, and a rooftop dinner at Lincoln Center. Because we fund arts, narrative, and cultural strategies for social change, these are often related to our work, but they are also key opportunities for bonding and enjoyment.

Over the years, the Asian Women Giving Circle has embraced a few annual traditions that we and our community have come to love. We start our year in September with a Garden Party in which we welcome all new grantee partners to the AWGC family. It's not a fundraiser—it's just an intimate gathering with food and beverage. Steering members come and a few of us invite a friend. It's relaxed, informal, and perfect for community building.

For about ten years, we hosted a "Sip, Shop, Swap" event, with the idea being that most of us had something nice in our closet that we no longer used. The event was a modest fundraiser that comprised a silent auction of the items donated, tasty appetizers, and lots of mingling. The "sip" portion was a curated wine tasting taught by one of our members who is a sommelier. We were happy to make $2,000. We've since let go of this event (not everything has to be a forever tradition!), but our sister circle in Dallas, the Orchid Giving Circle, took the idea and ran with it. Their closets are clearly better than ours because year one, they raised $10,000.

We end our year in May or June with a Celebration of Arts and Activism. This is our annual fundraising event and we usually do only one of these a year because events are a lot of work. And we try to keep it fairly low-key because that is our group's personality. We invite our community of donors, doers, and artists activists to come together to celebrate Asian American women and gender-expansive folks who are making equitable social change via narrative and cultural strategies. We ask a few grantee partners to share their work (with honoraria of course), keep remarks to a minimum, and make sure there's lots of good food (often dim sum) and wine.

In addition to giving shape to the year or offering an opportunity to fundraise, a party or event can also be a way to introduce folks who might not otherwise get together. The Women's Giving Alliance spans a large geographic range in the greater Jacksonville, Florida, area, and their size means that many members don't know each other well. To help with this, they organize twice-a-year zip code events, which might take the form of a cocktail party or a zoo outing or a gathering at a restaurant. The only point of these is to socialize and get to know each other better, especially those who live close by. It's a neighborhood-by-neighborhood way of knitting together a larger group.

On the other side of the country, the Latino Community Foundation is a network of Latinx circles up and down the great state of California. They host an annual convening that's like a conference married to a homecoming. It's galvanizing and nurturing for the circles in this network to get the boost of connecting to the larger mission and vision of the organization. Community Investment Network hosts an annual national get-together as well and they've figured out a way to make it informative, meaningful, and fun. Going to their annual meetings feels like getting a boost of vitamin C, or a bump of oxytocin, the "feel good" hormone.

Philanthropy can sometimes be performative, status-driven, or full of virtue-signaling. Groups of people doing philanthropy together have a built-in mechanism for having a good time, and that is each other. Getting to know each other deeply and enjoying each other's company while you're doing good for your community makes the bonds of collective action that much stronger.

Longtime community organizers know the number one most important thing is building authentic relationships with each other and with community members, and that's because trust is so important when doing sometimes difficult, even dangerous, work together. Relationship building is foundational, and elements include being there, being in the same room, listening, sharing, having the courage to be vulnerable, and sticking around for a while. It may seem obvious, but in order to identify what issues concern people, we have to be curious and listen to them, which requires being there and at least some trust. In order to figure out what might address those concerns, we've got to engage, listen, talk, argue, strategize—all of which require being in relationships and deepening them.

I LIVED FOR a year in Thailand after college to study Buddhism and explore the world and myself. As part of that project, I spent two weeks at a silent meditation retreat in the forest. I fell asleep during every single 4 a.m. meditation session. I was mortified to learn that I was so resistant to the hours and hours of meditation, which involves deeply letting go and giving in, that I spent the first two full days gossiping *in my own head* about the other participants . . . I wonder if that cute boy is dating that cute girl . . . maybe that guy is from Australia . . . those two girls are definitely talking (against the rules) . . . I love her sarong . . . how are we going to bathe? . . . I fear there are bugs in my bed . . . I wonder if that monk ever had a lover . . . I wonder what that monk's life was like before coming here . . . what's up with Mom and Dad at home, I wonder? I'm starving, what's for dinner . . .

Finally, almost in disgust, I gave up. I stopped making up stories about the other people in the room and started to pay attention to what was right in front of me, which was the temple (the *wat*, in Thai), the occasional instructions they fed us, how my knees ached from sitting cross-legged on the floor for hours, and yes, finally, on my breath.

The retreat was designed for Westerners, so although it's not really like a ladder, they taught us about certain "stages" we might notice in this meditation practice called *anapanasati*, which is a Pali word for "mindfulness of breathing." An early stage is called *piti*, which is a type of joy that feels bubbly, tingly, almost carbonated, buoyant. It feels amazing. The monks warned us that beginning meditators can get stuck in *piti* because it's so nice. As we practiced, we could get there, notice it, enjoy it, say hello, then keep on going.

Piti is just one aspect of joy. Joy can come in so many forms. There's the pure pleasure of getting in the zone, being so completely immersed in a book, painting, piece of music, or writing that you lose all sense of time. There's the quiet, content, total bliss of sitting in front of a fireplace with a loved one, drinking tea or a glass of wine, just being together. There's the laugh out loud, rocking hilarity of cracking up with buddies. There's the deep satisfaction of cooking a meal together, then sitting down to enjoy it. There's the joyful, bubbling, excited contentment of building something well. There's the bone-deep, settled, good feeling of a cuddle with my best boy (my dog), Stu. The satisfaction of doing some hard work, figuring out a conundrum, finally learning a new tricky knitting pattern, dancing, hitting a fantastic forehand, taking a walk outside, the beach—any beach—trying a new restaurant, discovering a new neighborhood, the wonder and privilege of seeing my children grow into adults, spending time with my aging parents, hanging out with Peter and our kids, seeing Stu run free, listening to a beautiful piece of music—all these things bring me joy, contentment, the feeling of deep immersion, the feeling of being deeply connected to nature, animals, humans, awe, aliveness, wonder, curiosity, hope. To me, these are all aspects of joy.

Joy is not unimportant, frivolous, ineffective, or easy. In fact, building in joy is a smart organizing strategy because it will keep people coming back to your thing, whether that's a cause, a job, a conference—or a giving circle. Who wants to go to a dreary meeting or conference? Mutual enjoyment is a crucial ligament in connecting us to our work and to each other. Fun can be raucous or quiet. It can feed introverts and extroverts alike. Joy feeds the mind, soul, heart, and body. I promise it will be worth the effort to think about what bits of fun you can include, and being open to ones that may surprise you, in the life of your giving circle, because over time, those bits of fun add up to joy.

It is particularly important to cultivate joy when doing this kind of work because it involves a large amount of vulnerability. Daring to open our hearts to one another, even sometimes in work settings. Getting to know each other, deeply and truly. Being courageous enough to be vulnerable and to witnessing someone else's vulnerability. Embracing surprises, coincidences, quirks, and whimsy, as companions to the work.

Jasmine Marrow, a senior program officer at the Bill & Melinda Gates Foundation, is a total delight. She's brilliant, quirky, kind, and wears the most excellent glasses. She shared her professional lineage with my team and hers during a Freedom School for Philanthropy cohort; she held the room rapt. She spoke of how Ida B. Wells "told the story of lynchings across the South to tell the stories that communities knew but didn't have the body of evidence to sit on, to support." And how James Baldwin "told hard truths. He used storytelling and imagination to change the stories of the world." Jasmine runs Data and Insights for a team within her behemoth of a foundation, and inspired by Ida B. Wells and James Baldwin, she aims to "lift up what's known and help it sit in a body of evidence."

When Jasmine was in high school, she and a group of buddies got a city bond measure passed. She was an AmeriCorps volunteer in East Palo Alto. Jasmine's mom always told her that kindness is free, even though her mother was not born to a kind family. Her dad, called "King Size," often said, "There but for the grace of God go I." She learned humility and grace from her family. She learned she had efficacy and could get meaningful things done. Jasmine also learned joy: "Joy is an often-overlooked emotion. It is not frivolous. It is so powerful. It is not easy. It is a choice, constantly. Joy can be the basis for revolution." Jas cultivates joy and whimsy in her personal and professional life, with friends, neighbors, and colleagues. Ask her about pet portraits, squirrel homes, holiday LEGOs, and snuzzle time. She says of herself, "In the best possible way, I am nobody special. And all of us 'nobody specials' can do amazing things."

Jasmine occupies an incredibly elevated and also incredibly difficult seat around the philanthropy social change table. She lives in the world of Big Phil, but is constantly trying to steer it toward something better. She navigates her role with integrity, intelligence, grace, humility, and a slightly oddball charming sense of humor. She is trying to change things, sensitively yet surely. The future of philanthropy rests with people like Jasmine, should it be so fortunate to get them.

Opening your heart to the quirks and surprises, to the possibilities of faith and human longing, to the possibility of heartbreak, to the deep appreciation of the "nobody specials"—this is part of the wonder, joy, poignancy, and occasional heartache of building belonging and yearning for something better. Of coming together in community to strive to make this world a better place. Of bridging ourselves and those around us to the Big We.

Be the We

The regrets tumbled in. Family emergency at Xin's in the Bronx. Angie and Andine were too tired, the week had been too long, they were just pooped. Kat got a last-minute audition in LA. Leslie and Pat were feeling under the weather. And worst of all, Melissa's family of four had norovirus and they share one bathroom.

But the rest of us gathered as planned at my kitchen table in Brooklyn. I'd defrosted and baked an eggplant parm. Peter lit a fire and put some chips in a bowl. I opened a bottle of wine. Joyce had picked up mailing labels and printed our annual appeal letters at the Ms. Foundation last week. Lisa and I gathered other random supplies and envelopes. She brought grapes and a large backpack to take letters to the mailbox. I'd ordered pretty stamps. Melinda, Shinhee, Helen, and Tiloma trundled in on this chilly, damp December day.

We sat, snacked, and talked. We signed letters, wrote notes, stuffed, stamped, and sealed our end-of-year fundraising letters. The Ms. Foundation for Women (our fiscal sponsor) is always surprised by how many snail-mailed donations our crowd sends in, so we do this annual, old-fashioned ritual year over year. Eighteen years running.

The conversation ranged. Lisa has resolved to eat more beans and get more exercise. That prompted the newly single Shinhee to enthusiastically share her new love of salsa and gyrotonics class. Which made a couple of us remember that time she fell while trying to show us a new turn—no injuries, much laughing. Which steered the conversation to health insurance because Andy quit his job, which meant Lisa's family was newly on the New York State Obamacare Exchange. So Melinda shared her family medical practice, which takes many health insurances, including the lowly ones. Speaking of cheap, Melinda's elderly mom is still scrounging free stuff, a frugality many of us can relate to. In fact, we're stickering over an old address so we can still use old stationery. When I gently suggested we recycle the 2017 stock, the group looked at me side-eyed, like "really?" so onward we go with our out-of-date stationery and labels. The holidays are upcoming so we shared family news. Helen works at CUNY, so we talked about the raging silencing of dissenting voices on the violence in Gaza. Some quiet, somber reflection. Which led some of us to remember our collegiate activism, and how for my generation, it was sit-ins in protest of South Africa's apartheid regime, for others it was opposition to wars in Vietnam or Iraq.

"It's nice here. Quiet," said Helen.

I've always enjoyed the rhythm, the semi-mindless yet also satisfying task of doing a mailing. Sign, decorate, fold, stuff, seal, stamp. Repeat a few hundred times. We know personally most of the people who add their dollars to our giving circle pot, so it's nice to remember them, wonder how they're doing, scribble a little note at the bottom, which is usually as simple as "hi to the fam!"

And I think we all appreciated the workaday solidarity of sitting at this kitchen table, doing a common task, in common purpose, for a larger social good.

We made plans to talk about our spring fundraiser later. And to gather the full group to meet early in the new year. And to watch football on Sunday. "Go Chiefs!" I cheered. (As a Kansas City gal and lifelong fan of our local team, I full-heartedly support Native American activists campaigning to change our team's iconography and name!) "Go Vikings!" added Shinhee. Not being a sports fan, Lisa said, "Wow. How? How odd."

WHEN I STARTED the AWGC in 2005, I thought the most important thing would be the money we moved into the world. There were, and still are, so few Asian American charities or philanthropic organizations. We were going to start an Asian American women's philanthropic vehicle! We'd move money! We'd add another dimension of Asian American womenness to the Asian American story!

I'm thrilled that we've raised and distributed $1.5 million into our communities over the past eighteen years. I'm so honored that we've been able to partner with over eighty amazing artist activists and be a small part of the work they've created and shared. But the thing that will endure, and that I think I'm most proud of, is our voice and our sisterhood.

It's funny that the artifacts that come to mind when I think about my dear sisters of the AWGC are all rather homey: Tupperware, the detritus of mailings like the one I just described, and my living room and kitchen table. My dog, Stu, makes himself comfortable in the middle of every party. He's an excellent plopper, sigher, and scrounger of cheese. My sisters of the AWGC have been over so often they know the routine. They walk in, give Stu a good belly rub, accept his gifts of shoes, take off their own shoes, put on slippers, then head straight to the kitchen. They unwrap what they've brought—clementines, grapes, noodles, leftovers, dumplings, cookies, seltzer, wine. Then we talk, nosh, and get to work.

Our belonging can be homey. It can be frivolous and fun. It can also be life-saving and life-affirming. We women of the AWGC have created a space where we're known, where we're regulars, where we belong. And that melding of the personal and the political is the alchemy of a giving circle.

TO THIS POINT in the book, I've asked you to ask yourself, on whose shoulders do you stand to do this work? From whom did you learn generosity—giving, sharing, helping one's neighbor? In these final pages, I'm asking you, what kind of ancestor do you want to be? What kind of legacy do you want to leave behind for your nieces, nephews, mentees, and heirs?

Moving from Me to We is about placing oneself in a lineage. There are "our people" who came before us, and there will be "our people" who come after us, with wonderful additions from folks from wildly different cultural heritages and life experiences. We've already thought about what we learn from our ancestors about mutual aid and lending a helping hand. Moving forward, what are the legacies of generosity we'd like to leave behind for the next generation, and the next seven generations about whom we can only dream?

This is my dream: Imagine a world in which millions of citizens are engaged in thousands of groups, meeting in each other's living rooms to put their heads and hearts together in order to better their neighborhoods and cities. They break bread together. They quarrel, listen, iterate, and learn together. They help each other out when someone is dealing with an ill parent or has a kid starting a new school. They volunteer, they vote, and they move money together.

Imagine it's you. You and your friends have been meeting in each other's living rooms for ten years now. You've been meeting half a dozen times per year, socializing, sharing news, and potlucking meals. You've also learned a lot about issues affecting your community. You've disagreed, laughed, talked, argued, hashed things out—for ten years. Together, you've moved thousands of dollars in support of unhoused folks in your community, or after-school programming for kids, or maybe for people escaping violence, or maybe to provide support for newcomers to this country, or maybe to support a local candidate or small business. You've kept learning, stayed interested, voted, activated, argued, and kept at it, together. You've celebrated each other's birthdays, weddings, and divorces. You've mourned loved ones who've died, and supported each other through illnesses, job losses, career changes, and elder care. You've lived a lot of life together. And you've done it in community with each other.

This is the world I want to live in. Let's get out there and build it—together.

• ACKNOWLEDGMENTS •

It's no surprise that it took a rather large Big We to get this book done.

I'd like to thank, first and foremost, the dozens of people who shared their stories with me. It was an incredible privilege, honor, and joy to witness, record, and now share their at-once ordinary and extraordinary lives. As you might imagine, the cutting room floor in this case is tragic. Even if your anecdotes aren't in these pages, the spirit of what you shared is imbued throughout. Thank you for your time, trust, and grace.

If philanthropy is a neighborhood, thank you to the cul-de-sac that is inhabited by these many wonderful colleagues. You have dared to cross into that liminal space that separates work friend from friend friend. We've shared and overshared, lifted beers and bourbons, had countless teas and coffees and so many oysters; we've met in living rooms, kitchens, dive bars, and even divier bars. Thank you to Kris Hermanns, Maria De La Cruz, Afi Tengue, Aparna Rae, Mario Lugay, Ricky Benavidez, Michael Pratt, CC Moore, Sara Lomelin, Marsha Morgan, Stephanie Fuerstner Gillis, Tricia Raikes, Jamia Wilson, Tony Bowen, Elaine Martyn, Tobi Becerra, Sudha Nandagopal, Makiyah Moody, Akruti Desai, Agus Galmarini, Jasmine Marrow, Sophie

Snowden, Andrew Dunckelman, Alex Jakana, Maheen Kaleem, Negar Tayyar, Leena Barakat, Donna Hall, Kashif Shaikh, Elaine Chu, Ada Williams Prince, Tuti B. Scott, Kristin Hayden, Darley Tom, Rena Greifinger, Virginia Wang, Aria Florant, and many more. Of karaoke special notes, thank you to Stephen Robinson, Efraín Gutiérrez, and Daniel Lee.

Thank you, deep thank-yous gam-saham-ni-da, to my Kitchen Table readers. Thank you to David Eng, Teemu Ruskola, and Shinhee Han for being critical friends and readers, but hewing to the nicer side of scary. To Daniel Lee and David Kyuman Kim, truly, you are my brothers from other mothers, and what fun for me to get to be a middle sister between you. Thank you to Shalini Somayaji, Sara Lomelin, Jasmine Marrow, Isis Krause, and Letarik Amare for being my first readers, chosen because of my deep respect for your intimate knowledge of our sector, but always guided by your heart and values of wanting it to be better.

To other and early readers and idea-brainstormers, Allison Fine, Margarethe Laurenzi, Paula Liang, and Heather McLeod Grant—thank you.

To my dear sisters of the Asian Women Giving Circle, thank you for the comradery, sisterhood, the many meals, laughs, inspiration, and kickass community-building and organizing. Thank you to Teresa Younger, Ellen Liu, and our sisters at the Ms. Foundation for Women for hosting us. To Ana Oliveira, Madeline Lamour Holder and the New York Women's Foundation, and Leena Barakat and Tamara Chao at the Women Donors Network, thank you for the community-rootedness you build and the powerful resource-moving you do.

Thank you to the Downtown Nasties for being steadfastly there, and huge kudos to the inspiration that is Melissa Walker and the States Project.

For under-the-hood help and repairs, thank you to Katherine A. Caldwell, and Aaron Shulman and Lauren Hamlin from Splash Literary.

To my agent, Maggie Cooper at Aevitas Creative Management, I adore the special sauce you bring, the art mixed with the commerce. This first-time author appreciates your "you got this" attitude, wisdom, occasional hand holding, and baked treats. I am so lucky you called me back. Thank you.

To my editor at Zando, Sarah Ried, thank the goddesses for you as well. I so appreciate your commonsense guidance, sharp and timely interventions, and general smarts, feedback, and bonhomie.

To Letarik Amare, Isis Krause, and Shalini Somayaji, Team Radiant, I do love you. Thank you for being my besties. I am so lucky to get to work with you every day. We have been through some fires and fractures together. Cheers to many more meals, beaches and mountains, rocks thrown into many more bodies of water, trips to Sephora, and holding that vision of the farm in our future.

To Mom, Dad, and Akka, my oldest and wisest readers, thank you.

And lastly, to my family, Alden, Maya, Magnus, for your invitations to spontaneous trips to Wegmans, the cocktails and meals made, the walks, all the holding down of the home fort and animals, for holding and caring for me, for laughter and keeping things in perspective, all of this meant the literal world to me. To Tina, Thea, Chris, Eli, and Rebecca, thank you for all the comforts that mean home. To my first, last, and always reader, Peter, thank you.

• BIBLIOGRAPHY •

Acoba, Elena. "Lily Messing: Outstanding Youth in Philanthropy." *Tucson Lifestyle*, November 14, 2022. https://www.tucsonlifestyle.com/local/lily-messing -outstanding-youth-in-philanthropy/article_25cddab6-6469-11ed-a431 -07009acbb8a0.html.

Alexandria Ocasio Cortez Campaign. *Mutual Aid 101*. March 2020. https://docs .google.com/document/d/e/2PACX-1vRMxVo9kdojzMdyOfapJUOB6Ko2 _1iAfIm8ELeIgma21wIt5HoTqP1QXadFo1eZcoySrPW6VtU_veyp/pub.

American Compass. "A Guide to Economic Inequality." Accessed August 1, 2024. https://americancompass.org/economic-inequality-guide/?gclid=CjwKCAjw _aemBhBLEiwAT98FMnGFXJBfUwYAIubzY7DQp67n4gGtmf9U6KKZC mcn7e5ccC_HQNkfUxoCrjYQAvD_BwE.

AmeriCorps. *Volunteering and Civic Life in America: Research Summary*. 2022. https://americorps.gov/sites/default/files/document/volunteering-civic-life -america-research-summary.pdf.

Anderson, D. Mark, and David Elsea. "The Meth Project and Teen Meth Use: New Estimates from the National and State Youth Risk Behavior Surveys." *Journal of Health Economics* 24, no. 12 (2015): 1644–1650. https://doi.org/10.1002/hec.3116.

Armah, Esther. Spoken address at Omega Women's Leadership Center: Women and Power Conference, October 2023.

Asian Women Giving Circle. "Asian Women Giving Circle Awards $81,000 in Grants in 2023." Accessed August 2, 2024. https://asianwomengivingcircle.org /projects/.

Baghai, Pooneh, Olivia Howard, Lakshmi Prakash, and Jill Zucker. "Women as the Next Wave of Growth in U.S. Wealth Management." *McKinsey and Company*, July 29, 2020. https://www.mckinsey.com/industries/financial-services/our -insights/women-as-the-next-wave-of-growth-in-us-wealth-management.

Bergdoll, Jon, Anna Pruitt, and Patrick Rooney. "U.S. Charitable Donations Fell to $499 Billion in 2022 as Stocks Slumped and Inflation Surged." *The Conversation*,

June 20, 2023. https://theconversation.com/us-charitable-donations-fell-to-49
9-billion-in-2022-as-stocks-slumped-and-inflation-surged-207688.

Blakely, Jason. "How School Choice Turns Education Into a Commodity." *The Atlantic*, April 17, 2017. https://www.theatlantic.com/education/archive/2017/04/is-school-choice-really-a-form-of-freedom/523089/.

Brest, Paul. "Strategic Philanthropy and Its Discontents." *Stanford Social Innovation Review*, April 27, 2015. https://ssir.org/up_for_debate/article/strategic_philanthropy_and_its_discontents#.

Brest, Paul, and Hal Harvey. *Money Well Spent: A Strategic Plan for Smart Philanthropy*. 2nd ed. Stanford: Stanford University Press, 2018.

Brous, Sharon. *The Amen Effect: Ancient Wisdom to Mend Our Broken Hearts and World*. New York: Penguin Random House, 2024.

———. "Train Yourself to Always Show Up." *New York Times*, January 19, 2024. https://www.nytimes.com/2024/01/19/opinion/religion-ancient-text-judaism.html?campaign_id=39&emc=edit_ty_20240119&instance_id=112926&nl=opinion-today&regi_id=74828348&segment_id=155752&te=1&user_id=b8c015625acf87b7c14d495e7b5f549e.

Bruni, Frank. "The Most Important Thing I Teach My Students Isn't on the Syllabus." *New York Times*, April 20, 2024. https://www.nytimes.com/2024/04/20/opinion/students-humility-american-politics.html.

C40 Knowledge Hub. "Sustainable Proximities." Accessed August 1, 2024. https://www.c40knowledgehub.org/s/sustainableproximities?language=en_US.

Cain, Jeff. "'Giving USA' Misses the Boat on the True State of Generosity in America." *Chronicle of Philanthropy*, July 26, 2023. https://www.philanthropy.com/article/giving-usa-misses-the-boat-on-the-true-state-of-generosity-in-america?utm_source=Iterable&utm_medium=email&utm_campaign=campaign_7356001_nl_Philanthropy-Today_date_20230727&cid=pt&source=ams&sourceid=&sra=true.

Charities Aid Foundation. "CAF World Giving Index 2022." Accessed August 1, 2024. https://www.cafonline.org/about-us/publications/2022-publications/caf-world-giving-index-2022#:~:text=The%20most%20generous%20country%20in,ever%20donated%20money%20in%202021.

Coalition for Asian American Children and Families. "18% and Growing Campaign." Accessed August 2, 2024. https://www.cacf.org/policy-advocacy/budget-equity-18-and-growing-campaign.

Colliver, Victoria. "California Statewide Study Investigates Causes and Impacts of Homelessness." *University of California San Francisco*, June 20, 2023. https://www.ucsf.edu/news/2023/06/425646/california-statewide-study-investigates-causes-and-impacts-homelessness.

Cooper, Sean. "What Happens When a Buffett Buys Your Town?" *Tablet*, July 13, 2021. https://www.tabletmag.com/sections/news/articles/buffett-kingston-sean-cooper.

Daily Freeman. "Here Are the Mid-Hudson Valley Organizations That Got NoVo Funding in 2021." *Daily Freeman*, February 6, 2023. https://www.dailyfreeman.com/2023/02/03/here-are-the-mid-hudson-valley-organizations-that-got-novo-funding-in-2021/.

Daniels, Alex. "The Brain Trust." *Chronicle of Philanthropy*, September 4, 2019. https://www.philanthropy.com/article/the-brain-trust/.

Davis, Carl, Emma Sifre, and Spandan Marasini. *The Geographic Distribution of Extreme Wealth in the U.S.* Institute on Tax and Economic Policy, October 2022. https://itep.org/the-geographic-distribution-of-extreme-wealth-in-the-u-s/#:~:text=%E2%96%B6%20More%20than%20one%20in,4.5%20trillion)%20held%20by%20billionaires.

Dennis, Elizabeth. "Women, Wealth and Investing – A Story of Evolution." *Morgan Stanley*, June 28, 2022. https://www.morganstanley.com/articles/female-invest-women-and-wealth#:~:text=Wealth%20Is%20Here-,Women%20investors%20are%20not%20a%20niche%20demographic%3B%20they're%20already,that%20baby%20boomers%20will%20possess.

Dickens, Charles. *A Christmas Carol.* Edited by Edmund Kemper Broadus. Chicago and New York: Scott, Foresman and Company, 1920.

Donors of Color Network. "The Apparitional Donor." Accessed August 1, 2024. https://www.donorsofcolor.org/resources/the-apparitional-donor.

Dumitru, Oana. "Half of Americans Say They Have Donated Money to Charity in the Past Year." *YouGov*, August 15, 2022. https://today.yougov.com/society/articles/43435-half-americans-donate-money-charity-past-year-poll.

Erceg-Hurn, David M. "Drugs, Money, and Graphic Ads: A Critical Review of the Montana Meth Project." *Prevention Science* 9, no. 4 (December 2008): 256-63. https://doi.org/10.1007/s11121-008-0098-5.

ESPN News Services. "NFL Averages 17.9M Viewers in 2023, Up 7% from Previous Year." *ESPN*, January 10, 2024. https://www.espn.com/nfl/story/_/id/39277615/nfl-averages-179m-viewers-2023-7-previous-year.

The Equitable Giving Lab. "The Women and Girls Index." Accessed July 30, 2024. https://equitablegivinglab.org/WGI/.

Fisher, Marc. "In Search of the Real Michelle Rhee." *Washington Post*, September 27, 2009. https://www.washingtonpost.com/wp-dyn/content/article/2009/09/23/AR2009092303309_2.html.

Garfield, Leanna. "Mark Zuckerberg Once Made a $100 Million Investment in a Major US City to Help Fix Its Schools – Now the Mayor Says the Effort

'Parachuted' In and Failed." *Business Insider*, May 12, 2018. https://www
.businessinsider.com/mark-zuckerberg-schools-education-newark-mayor-ras
-baraka-cory-booker-2018-5.

Gelles, David. "Billionaire No More: Patagonia Founder Gives Away the
Company." *New York Times*, September 14, 2022. https://www.nytimes.com/2022
/09/14/climate/patagonia-climate-philanthropy-chouinard.html.

Gessen, Masha. "The Prolific Activism of Urvashi Vaid." *New Yorker*, May 24,
2022. https://www.newyorker.com/news/postscript/the-prolific-activism-of
-urvashi-vaid.

Graff, Amy. "The Most Surprising Findings in a New Study on Homelessness in
California." *SFGATE*, June 20, 2023. https://www.sfgate.com/bayarea/article
/california-homelessness-study-surprising-findings-18161475.php.

Grose, Jessica. "What Churches Offer That 'Nones' Still Long For." *New York
Times*, June 28, 2023. https://www.nytimes.com/2023/06/28/opinion/religion
-affiliation-community.html?campaign_id=39&emc=edit_ty_20230628&instance
_id=96215&nl=opinion-today&regi_id=74828348&segment_id=137848&te
=1&user_id=b8c015625acf87b7c14d495e7b5f549e.

Gunther, Marc. "NoVo Fund, Led by a Buffett Son, Criticized for Staff and
Program Cuts." *Chronicle of Philanthropy*, May 19, 2020. https://www
.philanthropy.com/article/novo-fund-led-by-a-buffett-son-criticized-for-staff
-and-program-cuts?sra=true&cid=gen_sign_in.

HarperCollins. "Melissa Walker." Accessed August 2, 2024. https://www
.harpercollins.com/blogs/authors/melissa-walker-2015411640167.

Hatfield, Jenn, and Ted Van Green. "Most Americans Don't Closely Follow
Professional or College Sports." *Pew Research Center*, October 17, 2023. https://
www.pewresearch.org/short-reads/2023/10/17/most-americans-dont-closely
-follow-professional-or-college-sports/.

Horner, Usci. "Earth Is Our Only Shareholder as of Now." *IPSO*, August 15, 2022.
https://www.ispo.com/en/sustainability/living-sustainability-and-environmental
-protection-patagonia-becomes-foundation.

IP Staff. "Philanthropy Awards, 2020." *Inside Philanthropy*, December 30, 2020.
https://www.insidephilanthropy.com/home/2020/philanthropy-awards.

———. "Philanthropy Awards, 2018." *Inside Philanthropy*, January 2, 2019.
https://www.insidephilanthropy.com/home/2018/12/31/philanthropy-awards
-2018.

Jacobson, Luke, Ji Hoon Choi, Levi Herron, and Samantha Rich. "What
Democratic Lawmakers Have Done With Their Trifecta in the First 100 Days."
Michigan Daily, April 10, 2023. https://www.michigandaily.com/news
/government/michigan-democratic-trifecta-100-days/.

Kampfner, John. *The Rich: From Slaves to Super Yachts: A 2000-Year History*. London: Little Brown, 2014.

Kavate, Michael. "Foundation Assets Reach a Record $1.5 Trillion, Propelled by Investment Gains and Big Donors." *Inside Philanthropy*, January 29, 2024. https://www.insidephilanthropy.com/home/2024/1/29/foundation-assets-reach-a-record.

Kennedy, Brian, Alec Tyson, and Cary Funk. "Americans' Trust in Scientists, Other Groups Declines." *Pew Research Center*, August 2, 2024. https://www.pewresearch.org/science/2022/02/15/americans-trust-in-scientists-other-groups-declines/#:~:text=In%20the%20latest%20survey%2C%20just,said%20this%20in%20November%202020.

Kim, CeFaan. "Angry Parents Rally Against Plan to Do Away With SHSAT Specialized Admissions Testing." *ABC News*, September 6, 2024. https://abc7ny.com/shsat-queens-testing-admissions/5244488/.

Kotlowitz, Alex. "'The Prize,' by Dale Russakoff." Review of *The Prize: Who's In Charge of America's Schools?*, by Dale Russakoff. *New York Times*, August 19, 2015.

Kramer, Mark R. "Catalytic Philanthropy." *Stanford Social Innovation Review*, Fall 2009. https://ssir.org/articles/entry/catalytic_philanthropy.

Kristof, Nicholas. "We Know the Cure for Loneliness. So Why Do We Suffer?" *New York Times*, September 6, 2023. https://www.nytimes.com/2023/09/06/opinion/loneliness-epidemic-solutions.html?campaign_id=39&emc=edit_ty_20230909&instance_id=102159&nl=opinion-today&regi_id=74828348&segment_id=144300&te=1&user_id=b8c015625acf87b7c14d495e7b5f549e.

The Lancet. "What Has the Gates Foundation Done for Global Health?" *The Lancet* 373, no. 9675 (May 2009): 1577. https://doi.org/10.1016/S0140-6736(09)60885-0.

Lee, Hali. "Cultures of Generosity and Philanthropy Within Communities of Color." *PBS*, May 9, 2023. https://www.pbs.org/wnet/chasing-the-dream/2023/09/cultures-of-generosity-and-philanthropy-within-communities-of-color/.

Lilly Family School of Philanthropy. "GivingUSA: Total U.S. Charitable Giving Declines in 2022 to $499.33 Billion Following Two Years of Record Generosity." Indiana University, June 30, 2023. https://philanthropy.indianapolis.iu.edu/news-events/news/_news/2023/giving-usa-total-us-charitable-giving-declined-in-2022-to-49933-billion-following-two-years-of-record-generosity.html.

Lomelin, Sara. "Your Invitation to Disrupt Philanthropy." Filmed April 2022 in Vancouver, BC. TED video. https://www.ted.com/talks/sara_lomelin_your_invitation_to_disrupt_philanthropy?language=en.

Los Angeles Times Editorial Board. "Gates Foundation Failures Show Philanthropists Shouldn't Be Setting America's Public School Agenda." *Los*

Angeles Times, June 1, 2016. https://www.latimes.com/opinion/editorials/la-ed
-gates-education-20160601-snap-story.html.

Loson-Ceballos, A., and M. D. Layton. *In Abundance: An Analysis of the Thriving Landscape of Collective Giving in the U.S.* Dorothy A. Johnson Center for Philanthropy at Grand Valley State University and Philanthropy Together, 2024. https://johnsoncenter.org/wp-content/uploads/2024/04/in-abundance-an-analysis -of-the-thriving-landscape-of-collective-giving-in-the-u-s.pdf.

Meyer, Lily. "What We Gain From a Good-Enough Life." Review of *The Good-Enough Life*, by Avram Alpert. *The Atlantic*, August 18, 2022. https://www .theatlantic.com/books/archive/2022/08/good-enough-life-winnicott-avram -alpert-book/671110/.

Miller, Elizabeth. "Mutual Aid Groups Rushed to the Rescue During COVID-19." *New Mexico In Depth*, September 28, 2020. https://nmindepth .com/2020/mutual-aid-groups-rushed-to-the-rescue-during-covid-19/.

Ms. Foundation for Women. *Pocket Change: How Women and Girls of Color Do More With Less*. July 1, 2020. https://forwomen.org/resources/ pocket-change-report/.

Oliphant, J. Baxter. "Top Tax Frustrations for Americans: The Feeling That Some Corporations, Wealthy People Don't Pay Fair Share." *Pew Research Center*, April 7, 2023. https://www.pewresearch.org/short-reads/2023/04/07/top-tax -frustrations-for-americans-the-feeling-that-some-corporations-wealthy-people -dont-pay-fair-share/.

One in an ARMY. "The Purple Effect: BTS ARMY Help Raise $1 Million through Independent Charity Fundraisers." *Medium*, April 25, 2020. https:// oneinanarmy.medium.com/the-purple-effect-bts-army-help-raise-1-million -e87a646d8716.

Ortutay, Barbara. "TikTok Teens, K-Pop Fans Appear to Have Punked Trump's Tulsa Comeback Rally." *CBC*, June 22, 2020. https://www.cbc.ca/news /entertainment/trump-rally-tiktok-kpop-1.5621880.

Patriotic Millionaires. "About the Patriotic Millionaires." Accessed July 30, 2024. https://patrioticmillionaires.org/about/.

Pearl, Morris, Erica Payne, and The Patriotic Millionaires. *Tax the Rich! How Lies, Loopholes and Lobbyists Make the Rich Even Richer*. New York: The New Press, 2021.

Picchi, Aimee. "Why 200 Millionaires Want Higher Taxes: Inequality is 'Eating Our World Alive.'" *CBS News*, January 18, 2023. https://www.cbsnews.com/news /millionaires-higher-taxes-on-rich-davos-inequality/.

Pullella, Phillip. "Pope Blesses Those Everyone Loves to Hate – Tax Collectors." *Reuters*, January 31, 2022. https://www.reuters.com/world/europe/pope-blesses-those-everyone-loves-hate-tax-collectors-2022-01-31/.

Radiant. "Publications." Accessed August 1, 2024. https://www.radiantstrategies.co/reports.

Raikes Foundation. "Education." Accessed August 1, 2024. https://www.raikesfoundation.org/what-we-do/education.

Russakoff, Dale. "Assessing the $100 Million Upheaval of Newark's Public Schools." Interview by Terry Gross. *Fresh Air*, NPR, September 21, 2015. https://www.npr.org/2015/09/21/442183080/assessing-the-100-million-upheaval-of-newarks-public-schools.

———. *The Prize: Who's In Charge of America's Schools?* New York: Houghton Mifflin Harcourt, 2015.

Russell, Travis. "Budgets Are Moral Documents. Congress Should Treat Them Accordingly." *Jesuits*, September 27, 2021. https://www.jesuits.org/stories/budgets-are-moral-documents-congress-should-treat-them-accordingly/#:~:text=September%2027%2C%202021%20%E2%80%94%20Budgets%20are,another%2C%20especially%20for%20the%20vulnerable.

Sandler, Rachel. "The Wealthiest People in the U.S. Have Big Wallets. That Doesn't Mean They All Write Big Checks." *Forbes*, September 27, 2022. https://www.forbes.com/sites/rachelsandler/2022/09/27/the-forbes-philanthropy-score-2022-how-charitable-are-the-richest-americans/?sh=64538eca098.

Schmidt, Caitlin. "Tucson Teen Philanthropy Group Gives $25,000 to Nonprofits – So Far." *Tucson.com*, February 19, 2023. https://tucson.com/news/solutions/tucson-teen-philanthropy-group-gives-25-000-to-nonprofits-so-far/article_661495c-910d-11ed-aebe-17fb1e487046.html.

Scott, Dylan. "Cory Booker's Massive Overhaul of the Newark Schools, Explained." *Vox*, March 13, 2019. https://www.vox.com/policy-and-politics/2019/3/13/18223129/2020-presidential-candidates-policies-cory-booker-newark-schools-2020.

Seitz, Amanda. "Loneliness Poses Health Risks as Deadly as Smoking, U.S. Surgeon General Says." *PBS News*, May 2, 2023. https://www.pbs.org/newshour/health/loneliness-poses-health-risks-as-deadly-as-smoking-u-s-surgeon-general-says.

Sherry, Simon. "How Often Do Couples Really Have Sex?" *Psychology Today*, June 26, 2024. https://www.psychologytoday.com/us/blog/psymon-says/202303/how-often-do-couples-really-have-sex.

Siblis Research. "Total Market Value of the U.S. Stock Market." Accessed July 30, 2024. https://siblisresearch.com/data/us-stock-market-value/#:~:text=The%20total%20market%20capitalization%20of,(Jan%201st%2C%202024).

Sidebotham, Charlotte. "Good Enough Is Good Enough!" *The British Journal of General Practice* 67, no. 660 (2017): 311. https://doi.org/10.3399/bjgp17X691409.

The States Project. "Our 2022 Stories of Impact Report." Accessed August 2, 2024. https://statesproject.org/2022-stories-of-impact/.

———. "The States Project." Accessed August 3, 2024. https://statesproject.org/.

Strauss, Valerie. "Bill and Melinda Gates Have Spent Billions to Shape Education Policy. Now, They Say, They're 'Skeptical' of 'Billionaires' Trying to Do Just That." *Washington Post*, February 10, 2020. https://www.washingtonpost.com/education/2020/02/10/bill-melinda-gates-have-spent-billions-dollars-shape-education-policy-now-they-say-theyre-skeptical-billionaires-trying-do-just-that/.

———. "Bill Gates Spent Hundreds of Millions of Dollars to Improve Teaching. New Report Says It Was a Bust." *Washington Post*, June 29, 2018. https://www.washingtonpost.com/news/answer-sheet/wp/2018/06/29/bill-gates-spent-hundreds-of-millions-of-dollars-to-improve-teaching-new-report-says-it-was-a-bust/.

———. "Let's Review How Bill and Melinda Gates Spent Billions of Dollars to Change Public Education." *Washington Post*, May 5, 2021. https://www.washingtonpost.com/education/2021/05/05/what-bill-melinda-gates-did-to-education/.

———. "The Real Story: Why Mark Zuckerberg's $100 Million Gift to Newark Schools Was Announced on Oprah's Show." *Washington Post*, September 24, 2015. https://www.washingtonpost.com/news/answer-sheet/wp/2015/09/24/the-real-story-why-mark-zuckerbergs-100-million-gift-to-newark-schools-was-announced-on-oprahs-show/.

———. "To Trump's Education Pick, the U.S. Public School System Is a Dead End." *Washington Post*, December 21, 2016. https://www.washingtonpost.com/news/answer-sheet/wp/2016/12/21/to-trumps-education-pick-the-u-s-public-school-system-is-a-dead-end/.

Strawser, Colton C., and Melissa S. Brown. *The 2023 DAF Report*. Jenkintown: National Philanthropic Trust, 2023. https://www.nptrust.org/reports/daf-report/.

Tompkins, Lucy. "Evaluating the Effectiveness of the Montana Meth Project." *Montana Kaimin*, November 16, 2016. https://www.montanakaimin.com/news/evaluating-the-effectiveness-of-the-montana-meth-project/article_39f61954-ac5a-11e6-b695-bfd686efc470.html.

Travers, Julia. "'Heartbroken and Stunned.' NoVo's Program Upheaval Sows Anger and Uncertainty." *Inside Philanthropy*, May 19, 2020. https://www.insidephilanthropy.com/home/2020/5/19/heartbroken-and-stunned-novos-program-upheaval-amid-pandemic-sows-anger-and-uncertainty.

Uchitelle, Louis. "Lonely Bowlers, Unite: Mend the Social Fabric; A Political Scientist Renews His Alarm at the Erosion of Community Ties." *New York Times*,

May 6, 2000. https://www.nytimes.com/2000/05/06/arts/lonely-bowlers-unite -mend-social-fabric-political-scientist-renews-his-alarm.html.

United Nations. "The 17 Goals." Accessed August 1, 2024. https://sdgs.un.org/goals.

U.S. Congressional Budget Office. *The Distribution of Household Income, 2018.* August 2021. https://www.cbo.gov/system/files/2021-08/57061-Distribution -Household-Income.pdf.

U.S. Department of Education. "Estimate: Biden-Harris Student Debt Relief to Cost an Average of $30 Billion Annually Over Next Decade." September 29, 2022. https://www.ed.gov/news/press-releases/us-department-education-estimate -biden-harris-student-debt-relief-cost-average-30-billion-annually-over-next -decade#:~:text=Estimated%20Cost%20to%20the%20Federal%20Government &text=The%20Department%20estimates%20that%2C%20over,will%20be%20 roughly%20%24305%20billion.

———. "Fiscal Year 2010 Budget Summary." https://www.ed.gov/sites/ed/files /about/overview/budget/budget10/summary/10summary.pdf.

U.S. Department of Health and Human Services. *Our Epidemic of Loneliness and Isolation: The U.S. Surgeon General's Advisory on the Healing Effects of Social Connection and Community.* Washington, DC: U.S. Department of Health and Human Services, 2023. https://www.hhs.gov/sites/default/files/surgeon-general -social-connection-advisory.pdf.

Vallely, Paul. *Philanthropy: From Aristotle to Zuckerberg.* London: Bloomsbury Continuum, 2020.

Velez, Jennifer. "BTS, Big Hit Entertainment and the BTS Army Donate Over $2 Million to Black Lives Matter." *Grammy Awards,* June 8, 2020. https://www .grammy.com/news/bts-big-hit-entertainment-and-bts-army-donate-over-2 -million-black-lives-matter.

Wedge, Marilyn. "What Is a 'Good Enough Mother'?" *Psychology Today,* May 3, 2016. https://www.psychologytoday.com/us/blog/suffer-the-children/201605 /what-is-good-enough-mother.

Wikipedia. "2022 United States Federal Budget." Accessed July 30, 2024. https:// en.wikipedia.org/wiki/2022_United_States_federal_budget.

Winnicott, D. W. *The Child, the Family, and the Outside World.* London: Penguin, 1973.

Yeung, Peter. "Parisians Are Pledging Allegiance to the 'Republic of Super Neighbors.' They Must Bring Cheese." *New York Times,* August 30, 2023. https:// www.nytimes.com/2023/08/30/realestate/paris-cities-neighbors.html.

Zunz, Olivier. "Alexis De Tocqueville On Associations and Philanthropy." *HistPhil,* July 13, 2015. https://histphil.org/2015/07/13/alexis-de-tocqueville-on -associations-and-philanthropy/.

· ADDITIONAL RESOURCES ·

Armah, Esther. *Emotional Justice: A Roadmap for Racial Healing*. Oakland: Berrett-Koehler, 2022.

Bennett, Jessica. "What If Instead of Calling People Out, We Called Them In?: Prof. Loretta J. Ross Is Combating Cancel Culture with a Popular Class at Smith College." *New York Times*, November 19, 2020. https://www.nytimes.com/2020/11/19/style/loretta-ross-smith-college-cancel-culture.html.

Brody, Richard. "'Stop Making Sense' and the Transformative Power of Collaboration." *New Yorker*, September 19, 2023. https://www.newyorker.com/culture/the-front-row/stop-making-sense-and-the-transformative-power-of-collaboration.

Birdsong, Mia. *How We Show Up: Reclaiming Family, Friendship, and Community*. New York: Hachette, 2020.

Buchanon, Phil. *Giving Done Right: Effective Philanthropy and Making Every Dollar Count*. New York: Hachette, 2019.

Collier, Charles W. *Wealth in Families*. 3rd ed. Boston: Harvard University Press, 2012.

Gary, Tracy. *Inspired Philanthropy: Your Step-by-Step Guide to Creating a Giving Plan and Leaving a Legacy*. 3rd ed. San Francisco: Jossey-Bass, 2007.

Giridharadas, Anand. *Winners Take All: The Elite Charade of Changing the World*. New York: Alfred A. Knopf, 2018.

Hughes, David. *Who Owns the Wind?: Climate Crisis and the Hope of Renewable Energy*. New York: Verso, 2021.

Johnson, Ayana Elizabeth, and Katharine K. Wilkinson. *All We Can Save: Truth, Courage, and Solutions for the Climate Crisis*. New York: One World, 2020.

Kim, Michelle Mijung. *The Wake Up: Closing the Gap Between Good Intentions and Real Change*. New York: Hachette, 2021.

Kimmerer, Robin Wall. *Braiding Sweetgrass: Indigenous Wisdom, Scientific Knowledge and the Teachings of Plants*. Minneapolis: Milkweed Editions, 2013.

Lemann, Nicholas. "Would the World be Better Off Without Philanthropists?" *New Yorker*, May 23, 2022.

Lewis-Kraus, Gideon. "The Reluctant Prophet of Effective Altruism." *The New Yorker*, August 2022. https://www.newyorker.com/magazine/2022/08/15/the-reluctant-prophet-of-effective-altruism.

Lilly Family School of Philanthropy, Indiana University. *Giving USA 2023: The Annual Report on Philanthropy for the Year 2022*. June 20, 2023. https://philanthropy.indianapolis.iu.edu/news-events/news/_news/2023/giving-usa-total-us-charitable-giving-declined-in-2022-to-49933-billion-following-two-years-of-record-generosity.html.

Lindsay, Drew. "What Philanthropy Elites Can Learn from Appalachia: Community Superhero and 'Hillbilly Lesbian' L. B. Prevette Tells It Like It Is." *Chronicle of Philanthropy*, April 1, 2024. https://www.philanthropy.com/commons/what-philanthropy-elites-can-learn-from-appalachia?utm_campaign=cop&utm_source=20240402&utm_medium=social&utm_content=li&sra=true.

Madoff, Ray. *Immortality and the Law: The Rising Power of the American Dead*. New Haven: Yale University Press, 2010.

Madoff, Ray. "When Charitable Giving Doesn't Go to Charities." *Alliance*, June 6, 2023. https://www.alliancemagazine.org/feature/when-charitable-giving-doesnt-go-to-charities/.

Marantz, Andrew. "What Should You Do With an Oil Fortune?" *New Yorker*, August 7, 2023.

McGhee, Heather. *The Sum of Us: What Racism Costs Everyone and How We Can Prosper Together*. New York: One World, 2021.

Packer, George. *Last Best Hope: America in Crisis and Renewal*. New York: Farrar, Straus and Giroux, 2021.

Parker, Priya. *The Art of Gathering: How We Meet and Why It Matters*. New York: Riverhead Books, 2020.

Phillips, Steve. *How We Win the Civil War: Securing a Multiracial Democracy and Ending White Supremacy for Good*. New York: The New Press, 2022.

———. *Brown Is the New White: How the Demographic Revolution Has Created a New American Majority*. New York: The New Press, 2016.

Putnam, Robert. *Bowling Alone: The Collapse and Revival of American Community*. New York: Simon & Schuster, 2000. Revised 2020.

Radiant Strategies. *Freedom School for Philanthropy*. 2023. https://www.freedomschoolforphilanthropy.org/.

Reich, David. "A Charitable Sleight of Hand: Madoff Launches Effort to Fix the Wrongs of Donor Advised Funds." *Boston College Law School Magazine Online*, Winter 2017. https://lawmagazine.bc.edu/2017/01/a-charitable-sleight-of-hand/.

Reich, Rob. *Just Giving: Why Philanthropy Is Failing Democracy and How It Can Do Better*. Princeton: Princeton University Press, 2018.

Risher, Jen. *We Need to Talk: A Memoir About Wealth*. Pasadena: Xeno Books, 2020.

Saunders-Hastings, Emma. *Private Virtues, Public Vices: Philanthropy and Democratic Equality*. Chicago: University of Chicago Press, 2022.

Schiller, Amy. *The Price of Humanity: How Philanthropy Went Wrong and How to Fix It*. New York: Melville House, 2023.

Stevenson, Bryan. *Just Mercy: A Story of Justice and Redemption*. New York: Spiegel & Grau, 2014.

Villanueva, Edgar. *Decolonizing Wealth: Indigenous Wisdom to Heal Divides and Restore Balance*. Oakland: Berrett-Koehler, 2018.

Wilkerson, Isabel. *Caste: The Origins of Our Discontents*. New York: Random House, 2020.

• ENDNOTES •

INTRODUCTION

1. Paul Brest and Hal Harvey, *Money Well Spent: A Strategic Plan for Smart Philanthropy*, 2nd ed. (Stanford: Stanford University Press, 2018).
2. I shared this story in an article published by my local PBS affiliate, WNET, in 2023: Lee, "Cultures of Generosity and Philanthropy Within Communities of Color," PBS, May 9, 2023, https://www.pbs.org/wnet /chasing-the-dream/2023/09/cultures-of-generosity-and-philanthropy -within-communities-of-color/.
3. Olivier Zunz, "Alexis De Tocqueville On Associations and Philanthropy," HistPhil, July 13, 2015, https://histphil.org/2015/07/13/alexis-de -tocqueville-on-associations-and-philanthropy/.
4. A. Loson-Ceballos and M. D. Layton, *In Abundance: An Analysis of the Thriving Landscape of Collective Giving in the U.S.*, Dorothy A. Johnson Center for Philanthropy at Grand Valley State University and Philanthropy Together, 2024, https://johnsoncenter.org/wp-content/uploads/2024/04 /in-abundance-an-analysis-of-the-thriving-landscape-of-collective-giving -in-the-u-s.pdf.

CHAPTER ONE

1. Dale Russakoff, *The Prize: Who's In Charge of America's Schools?* (New York: Houghton Mifflin Harcourt, 2015), 3.
2. Russakoff, *The Prize*, 27.
3. Russakoff, *The Prize*, 29.
4. Valerie Strauss, "The Real Story: Why Mark Zuckerberg's $100 Million Gift to Newark Schools Was Announced on Oprah's Show," *Washington Post*, September 24, 2015, https://www.washingtonpost.com/news/answer -sheet/wp/2015/09/24/the-real-story-why-mark-zuckerbergs-100-million -gift-to-newark-schools-was-announced-on-oprahs-show/.

5. Marc Fisher, "In Search of the Real Michelle Rhee," *Washington Post*, September 27, 2009, https://www.washingtonpost.com/wp-dyn/content /article/2009/09/23/AR2009092303309_2.html.

6. Jason Blakely, "How School Choice Turns Education Into a Commodity," *The Atlantic*, April 17, 2017, https://www.theatlantic.com/education /archive/2017/04/is-school-choice-really-a-form-of-freedom/523089/.

7. Valerie Strauss, "To Trump's Education Pick, the U.S. Public School System Is a Dead End," *Washington Post*, December 21, 2016, https://www .washingtonpost.com/news/answer-sheet/wp/2016/12/21/to-trumps -education-pick-the-u-s-public-school-system-is-a-dead-end/.

8. Blakely, "School Choice."

9. U.S. Department of Education, "Fiscal Year 2010 Budget Summary." https://www.ed.gov/sites/ed/files/about/overview/budget/budget10 /summary/10summary.pdf.

10. Alex Kotlowitz, "'The Prize,' by Dale Russakoff," review of *The Prize: Who's In Charge of America's Schools?*, by Dale Russakoff, *New York Times*, August 19, 2015.

11. Russakoff, *The Prize*, 153.

12. Dale Russakoff, "Assessing the $100 Million Upheaval of Newark's Public Schools," interview by Terry Gross, *Fresh Air*, NPR, September 21, 2015, https://www.npr.org/2015/09/21/442183080/assessing-the-100-million -upheaval-of-newarks-public-schools.

13. Russakoff, interview.

14. Russakoff, interview.

15. Leanna Garfield, "Mark Zuckerberg Once Made a $100 Million Investment in a Major US City to Help Fix Its Schools—Now the Mayor Says the Effort 'Parachuted' In and Failed," *Business Insider*, May 12, 2018, https://www.businessinsider.com/mark-zuckerberg-schools-education -newark-mayor-ras-baraka-cory-booker-2018-5.

16. Russakoff, *The Prize*, 220.

17. Dylan Scott, "Cory Booker's Massive Overhaul of the Newark Schools, Explained," *Vox*, March 13, 2019, https://www.vox.com/policy-and-politics /2019/3/13/18223129/2020-presidential-candidates-policies-cory-booker -newark-schools-2020.

18. Paul Vallely, *Philanthropy: From Aristotle to Zuckerberg* (London: Bloomsbury Continuum, 2020), 459.

19. Vallely, *Philanthropy*, 459.

20. Valerie Strauss, "Bill Gates Spent Hundreds of Millions of Dollars to Improve Teaching. New Report Says It Was a Bust," *Washington Post*, June 29, 2018, https://www.washingtonpost.com/news/answer-sheet/wp/2018 /06/29/bill-gates-spent-hundreds-of-millions-of-dollars-to-improve -teaching-new-report-says-it-was-a-bust/.

21. Valerie Strauss, "Bill and Melinda Gates Have Spent Billions to Shape Education Policy. Now, They Say, They're 'Skeptical' of 'Billionaires' Trying to Do Just That," *Washington Post*, February 10, 2020, https://www .washingtonpost.com/education/2020/02/10/bill-melinda-gates-have -spent-billions-dollars-shape-education-policy-now-they-say-theyre -skeptical-billionaires-trying-do-just-that/; Valerie Strauss, "Let's Review How Bill and Melinda Gates Spent Billions of Dollars to Change Public Education," *Washington Post*, May 5, 2021, https://www.washingtonpost .com/education/2021/05/05/what-bill-melinda-gates-did-to-education/.

22. Los Angeles Times Editorial Board, "Gates Foundation Failures Show Philanthropists Shouldn't Be Setting America's Public School Agenda," *Los Angeles Times*, June 1, 2016, https://www.latimes.com/opinion/editorials /la-ed-gates-education-20160601-snap-story.html.

23. Vallely, *Philanthropy*, 484.

24. Vallely, *Philanthropy*, 484.

25. Vallely, *Philanthropy*, 487.

26. The Lancet, "What Has the Gates Foundation Done for Global Health?," *The Lancet* 373, no. 9675 (May 2009): 1577. https://doi.org/10.1016 /S0140-6736(09)60885-0.

27. Vallely, *Philanthropy*, 497–98.

28. Vallely, *Philanthropy*, 502.

29. Mark R. Kramer, "Catalytic Philanthropy," *Stanford Social Innovation Review*, Fall 2009, https://ssir.org/articles/entry/catalytic_philanthropy.

30. Kate Zernike, "With Scenes of Blood and Pain, Ads Battle Methamphetamine in Montana," *New York Times*, February 26, 2006, https://www.nytimes.com/2006/02/26/us/with-scenes-of-blood-and-pain -ads-battle-methamphetamine-in-montana.html.

31. Lucy Tompkins, "Evaluating the Effectiveness of the Montana Meth Project," *Montana Kaimin*, November 16, 2016, https://www .montanakaimin.com/news/evaluating-the-effectiveness-of-the-montana -meth-project/article_39f61954-ac5a-11e6-b695-bfd686efc470.html.

32. David M. Erceg-Hurn, "Drugs, Money, and Graphic Ads: A Critical Review of the Montana Meth Project," *Prevention Science* 9, no. 4 (December 2008): 256–63, https://doi.org/10.1007/s11121-008-0098-5.

33. D. Mark Anderson, "Does Information Matter? The Effect of the Meth Project on Meth Use among Youths," *Journal of Health Economics* 29, no. 5 (2010): 732–742, https://doi.org/10.1016/j.jhealeco.2010.06.005.

34. D. Mark Anderson and David Elsea, "The Meth Project and Teen Meth Use: New Estimates from the National and State Youth Risk Behavior Surveys," *Journal of Health Economics* 24, no. 12 (2015): 1644–1650, https:// doi.org/10.1002/hec.3116.

35. Kramer, "Catalytic Philanthropy."

36. There's a lot to critique about wealthy people parking money into private foundations and DAFs. The money has been set aside for charitable purposes, but if it's sitting in one of these vehicles, it's not actually doing any social good in the world. There isn't a public good being done in exchange for the tax deduction the wealthy person received. Boston College professor Ray Madoff has written extensively about this issue.

37. Rachel Sandler, "The Wealthiest People in the U.S. Have Big Wallets. That Doesn't Mean They All Write Big Checks," *Forbes*, September 27, 2022, https://www.forbes.com/sites/rachelsandler/2022/09/27/the-forbes-philanthropy-score-2022-how-charitable-are-the-richest-americans/?sh=645381eca098.

38. "The Women and Girls Index," The Equitable Giving Lab, accessed July 30, 2024, https://equitablegivinglab.org/WGI/.

39. Ms. Foundation for Women, *Pocket Change: How Women and Girls of Color Do More With Less*, July 1, 2020, https://forwomen.org/resources/pocket-change-report/.

40. Julia Travers, "'Heartbroken and Stunned.' NoVo's Program Upheaval Sows Anger and Uncertainty," *Inside Philanthropy*, May 19, 2020, https://www.insidephilanthropy.com/home/2020/5/19/heartbroken-and-stunned-novos-program-upheaval-amid-pandemic-sows-anger-and-uncertainty.

41. Marc Gunther, "NoVo Fund, Led by a Buffett Son, Criticized for Staff and Program Cuts," *Chronicle of Philanthropy*, May 19, 2020, https://www.philanthropy.com/article/novo-fund-led-by-a-buffett-son-criticized-for-staff-and-program-cuts?sra=true&cid=gen_sign_in.

42. IP Staff, "Philanthropy Awards, 2020," *Inside Philanthropy*, December 30, 2020, https://www.insidephilanthropy.com/home/2020-philanthropy-awards; Full disclosure, I was part of a team that won "Donor Organizers of the Year" in 2018 for our donors of color research and network build: "Philanthropy Awards, 2018," *Inside Philanthropy*, January 2, 2019, https://www.insidephilanthropy.com/home/2018/12/31/philanthropy-awards-2018.

43. Gunther, "NoVo Fund."

44. National Philanthropic Trust, *The 2023 DAF Report*, https://www.nptrust.org/reports/daf-report/.

45. "Here Are the Mid-Hudson Valley Organizations That Got NoVo Funding in 2021," *Daily Freeman*, February 6, 2023, https://www.dailyfreeman.com/2023/02/03/here-are-the-mid-hudson-valley-organizations-that-got-novo-funding-in-2021/.

46. Sean Cooper, "What Happens When a Buffett Buys Your Town?," *Tablet*, July 13, 2021, https://www.tabletmag.com/sections/news/articles/buffett-kingston-sean-cooper.

47. Cooper, "Buffett."

48. Cooper, "Buffett."

49. Cooper, "Buffett."

50. Michael Kavate, "Foundation Assets Reach a Record $1.5 Trillion, Propelled by Investment Gains and Big Donors," *Inside Philanthropy*, January 29, 2024, https://www.insidephilanthropy.com/home/2024/1/29/foundation-assets-reach-a-record.

51. David Gelles, "Billionaire No More: Patagonia Founder Gives Away the Company," *New York Times*, September 14, 2022, https://www.nytimes.com/2022/09/14/climate/patagonia-climate-philanthropy-chouinard.html.

52. Usci Horner, "Earth Is Our Only Shareholder as of Now," *IPSO*, August 15, 2022, https://www.ispo.com/en/sustainability/living-sustainability-and-environmental-protection-patagonia-becomes-foundation.

53. "About the Patriotic Millionaires," Patriotic Millionaires, accessed July 30, 2024, https://patrioticmillionaires.org/about/.

54. Morris Pearl, Erica Payne, and The Patriotic Millionaires, *Tax the Rich! How Lies, Loopholes and Lobbyists Make the Rich Even Richer* (New York: The New Press, 2021).

55. Phillip Pullella, "Pope Blesses Those Everyone Loves to Hate—Tax Collectors," *Reuters*, January 31, 2022, https://www.reuters.com/world/europe/pope-blesses-those-everyone-loves-hate-tax-collectors-2022-01-31/.

56. Lilly Family School of Philanthropy, "GivingUSA: Total U.S. Charitable Giving Declines in 2022 to $499.33 Billion Following Two Years of Record Generosity," *Indiana University*, June 30, 2023, https://philanthropy.indianapolis.iu.edu/news-events/news/_news/2023/giving-usa-total-us-charitable-giving-declined-in-2022-to-49933-billion-following-two-years-of-record-generosity.html.

57. "2022 United States Federal Budget," Wikipedia, accessed July 30, 2024, https://en.wikipedia.org/wiki/2022_United_States_federal_budget.

58. "Total Market Value of the U.S. Stock Market," Siblis Research, accessed July 30 2024, https://siblisresearch.com/data/us-stock-market-value/#:~:text=The%20total%20market%20capitalization%20of,(Jan%201st%2C%202024).

59. 150 lbs vs 3,000 lbs vs 15,000 lbs.

60. J. Baxter Oliphant, "Top Tax Frustrations for Americans: The Feeling That Some Corporations, [sic] Wealthy People Don't Pay Fair Share," *Pew Research Center*, April 7, 2023, https://www.pewresearch.org/short-reads/2023/04/07/top-tax-frustrations-for-americans-the-feeling-that-some-corporations-wealthy-people-dont-pay-fair-share/.

61. "A Guide to Economic Inequality," American Compass, accessed August 1, 2024, https://americancompass.org/economic-inequality-guide/?gclid=CjwKCAjw_aemBhBLEiwAT98FMnGFXJBfUwYAIubzY7DQp67n4gGtmf9U6KKZCmcn7e5ccC_HQNkfUxoCrjYQAvD_BwE.

62. U.S. Congressional Budget Office, *The Distribution of Household Income, 2018*, August 2021, https://www.cbo.gov/system/files/2021-08/57061 -Distribution-Household-Income.pdf.

63. "Gini Index: United States," World Bank Group, accessed August 1, 2024, https://data.worldbank.org/indicator/SI.POV.GINI?locations=US& most_recent_value_desc=false.

64. Aimee Picchi, "Why 200 Millionaires Want Higher Taxes: Inequality Is 'Eating Our World Alive,'" *CBS News*, January 18, 2023, https://www .cbsnews.com/news/millionaires-higher-taxes-on-rich-davos-inequality/.

65. U.S. Department of Education, *Estimate: Biden-Harris Student Debt Relief to Cost an Average of $30 Billion Annually Over Next Decade*, September 29, 2022, https://www.ed.gov/news/press-releases/us-department-education -estimate-biden-harris-student-debt-relief-cost-average-30-billion -annually-over-next-decade#:~:text=Estimated%20Cost%20to%20the%20 Federal%20Government&text=The%20Department%20estimates%20 that%2C%20over,will%20be%20roughly%20%20%24305%20billion. There are lots of good arguments that canceling student debt would help the economy because there would be more people able to participate in it, like by buying homes. Also, since folks of color hold more student debt, alleviating some of that would go a ways toward ameliorating the racial wealth gap.

66. The full list of 17 SDG goals: 1) End poverty in all its forms everywhere; 2) End hunger, achieve food security and improved nutrition, and promote sustainable agriculture; 3) Ensure healthy lives and promote well-being for all at all ages; 4) Ensure inclusive and equitable quality education and promote lifelong learning opportunities for all; 5) Achieve gender equality and empower all women and girls; 6) Ensure availability and sustainable management of clean water and sanitation for all; 7) Ensure access to affordable, reliable, and sustainable energy for all; 8) Promote sustained, inclusive, and sustainable economic growth, full and productive employment, and decent work for all; 9) Build resilient infrastructure, promote inclusive and sustainable Industrialization, and foster innovation; 10) Reduce inequality within and among countries; 11) Make cities and human settlements inclusive, safe, resilient, and sustainable; 12) Ensure sustainable consumption and production patterns; 13) Take urgent action to combat climate change and its impacts; 14) Life below the water: Conserve and sustainably use the oceans, seas, and marine resources for sustainable development; 15) Life on land: Protect, restore, and promote sustainable use of terrestrial ecosystems, sustainably manage forests, combat desertification, and halt and reverse land degradation and halt biodiversity loss; 16) Promote peaceful and inclusive societies for sustainable development, provide access to justice for all, and build effective, accountable, and inclusive institutions at all levels; 17) Strengthen

the means of implementation and revitalize the Global Partnerships for Sustainable Development. See "The 17 Goals," United Nations, accessed August 1, 2024, https://sdgs.un.org/goals.

CHAPTER TWO

1. Houses of worship have raised money for millennia but the rise of a professionalized philanthropy sector, supported by tax codes and other structures, begins here.

2. "CAF World Giving Index 2022," Charities Aid Foundation, accessed August 1, 2024, https://www.cafonline.org/about-us/publications/2022 -publications/caf-world-giving-index-2022#:~:text=The%20most%20 generous%20country%20in,ever%20donated%20money%20in%202021.

3. Oana Dumitru, "Half of Americans Say They Have Donated Money to Charity in the Past Year," *YouGov*, August 15, 2022, https://today.yougov .com/society/articles/43435-half-americans-donate-money-charity-past -year-poll.

4. AmeriCorps, *Volunteering and Civic Life in America: Research Summary*, 2022, https://americorps.gov/sites/default/files/document/volunteering -civic-life-america-research-summary.pdf.

5. Jenn Hatfield and Ted Van Green, "Most Americans Don't Closely Follow Professional or College Sports," *Pew Research Center*, October 17, 2023, https://www.pewresearch.org/short-reads/2023/10/17/most-americans -dont-closely-follow-professional-or-college-sports/; ESPN News Services, "NFL Averages 17.9M Viewers in 2023, Up 7% from Previous Year," ESPN, January 10, 2024, https://www.espn.com/nfl/story/_/id/39277615 /nfl-averages-179m-viewers-2023-7-previous-year; Simon Sherry, "How Often Do Couples Really Have Sex?," *Psychology Today*, June 26, 2024, https://www.psychologytoday.com/us/blog/psymon-says/202303 /how-often-do-couples-really-have-sex.

6. Jon Bergdoll, Anna Pruitt, and Patrick Rooney, "U.S. Charitable Donations Fell to $499 Billion in 2022 as Stocks Slumped and Inflation Surged," *The Conversation*, June 20, 2023, https://theconversation.com/us-charitable -donations-fell-to-499-billion-in-2022-as-stocks-slumped-and-inflation -surged-207688.

7. Lilly Family School of Philanthropy, "GivingUSA."

8. Carl Davis, Emma Sifre, Spandan Marasini, *The Geographic Distribution of Extreme Wealth in the U.S.,* Institute on Tax and Economic Policy, October 2022, https://itep.org/the-geographic-distribution-of-extreme-wealth-in -the-u-s/.

9. The GivingUSA report leaves out a great deal, especially the macro contexts in which giving appears to have fallen, like the Great Recession, COVID, wars, and the ways in which people give outside of the 501(c)(3) context;

for instance, Jeff Cain, "'Giving USA' Misses the Boat on the True State of Generosity in America," *Chronicle of Philanthropy*, July 26, 2023, https://www.philanthropy.com/article/giving-usa-misses-the-boat-on-the-true-state-of-generosity-in-america?utm_source=Iterable&utm_medium=email&utm_campaign=campaign_7356001_nl_Philanthropy-Today_date_20230727&cid=pt&source=ams&sourceid=&sra=true.

10. Masha Gessen, "The Prolific Activism of Urvashi Vaid," *New Yorker*, May 24, 2022, https://www.newyorker.com/news/postscript/the-prolific-activism-of-urvashi-vaid.

11. Gessen, "Urvashi Vaid."

12. You can download the full report at the Donors of Color Network website: "The Apparitional Donor," Donors of Color Network, accessed August 1, 2024, https://www.donorsofcolor.org/resources/the-apparitional-donor.

13. If you'd like to geek out, you can read *Philanthropy Always Sounds Like Someone Else: A Portrait of High Net Worth Donors of Color* on the "Publications" section of my website, Radiant, https://www.radiantstrategies.co/reports.

14. Jorge is referencing the book *Auntie Mame* by Patrick Dennis.

15. I asked people to describe their race, ethnicity, and other identities in their own words and I've respected their preferences here.

16. Watch her TED talk here: Sara Lomelin, "Your Invitation to Disrupt Philanthropy," filmed April 2022 in Vancouver, BC, TED video, https://www.ted.com/talks/sara_lomelin_your_invitation_to_disrupt_philanthropy?language=en.

CHAPTER THREE

1. Esther Armah, spoken address at Omega Women's Leadership Center: Women and Power conference, October 2023.

2. For a defense of strategic philanthropy see, for instance, Paul Brest, "Strategic Philanthropy and Its Discontents," *Stanford Social Innovation Review*, April 27, 2015, https://ssir.org/up_for_debate/article/strategic_philanthropy_and_its_discontents#.

3. Vallely, *Philanthropy*, 338–39.

4. John Kampfner, *The Rich: From Slaves to Super Yachts: A 2000-Year History* (London: Little Brown, 2014), 233.

5. She said this at a meeting of the Impact Driven Philanthropy Collaborative, in September 2022.

6. "Education," Raikes Foundation, accessed August 1, 2024, https://www.raikesfoundation.org/what-we-do/education.

7. Alex Daniels, "The Brain Trust," *Chronicle of Philanthropy*, September 4, 2019, https://www.philanthropy.com/article/the-brain-trust/.

8. Daniels, "Brain Trust."

CHAPTER FOUR

1. U.S. Department of Health and Human Services, *Our Epidemic of Loneliness and Isolation: The U.S. Surgeon General's Advisory on the Healing Effects of Social Connection and Community* (Washington, DC: U.S. Department of Health and Human Services, 2023), https://www.hhs.gov /sites/default/files/surgeon-general-social-connection-advisory.pdf.

2. Nicholas Kristof, "We Know the Cure for Loneliness. So Why Do We Suffer?," *New York Times*, September 6, 2023, https://www.nytimes.com /2023/09/06/opinion/loneliness-epidemic-solutions.html?campaign_id =39&emc=edit_ty_20230909&instance_id=102159&nl=opinion-today &regi_id=74828348&segment_id=144300&te=1&user_id=b8c015625acf8 7b7c14d495e7b5f549e.

3. Charles Dickens, *A Christmas Carol*, ed. Edmund Kemper Broadus (Chicago and New York: Scott, Foresman and Company, 1920).

4. Louis Uchitelle, "Lonely Bowlers, Unite: Mend the Social Fabric; A Political Scientist Renews His Alarm at the Erosion of Community Ties," *New York Times*, May 6, 2000, https://www.nytimes.com/2000/05/06/arts /lonely-bowlers-unite-mend-social-fabric-political-scientist-renews-his -alarm.html.

5. Amanda Seitz, "Loneliness Poses Health Risks as Deadly as Smoking, U.S. Surgeon General Says," *PBS News*, May 2, 2023, https://www.pbs.org /newshour/health/loneliness-poses-health-risks-as-deadly-as-smoking -u-s-surgeon-general-says.

6. Kristof, "Cure for Loneliness."

7. Kristof, "Cure for Loneliness."

8. "Sustainable Proximities," C40 Knowledge Hub, accessed August 1, 2024, https://www.c40knowledgehub.org/s/sustainableproximities?language =en_US.

9. Peter Yeung, "Parisians Are Pledging Allegiance to the 'Republic of Super Neighbors.' They Must Bring Cheese," *New York Times*, August 30, 2023, https://www.nytimes.com/2023/08/30/realestate/paris-cities-neighbors .html.

10. Ian Leslie, "Why Your 'Weak-Tie' Friendships May Mean More Than You Think," BBC, July 2, 2020, https://www.bbc.com/worklife/article/2020 0701-why-your-weak-tie-friendships-may-mean-more-than-you-think.

11. Mark S. Granovetter, "The Strength of Weak Ties," American Journal of Sociology 78, no. 6 (May 1973): 1360–1380, https://doi.org/10.1086 /225469.

12. Gillian M. Sandstrom and Elizabeth W. Dunn, "Social Interactions and Well-Being: The Surprising Power of Weak Ties," Personality and Social Psychology Bulletin 40, no. 7 (2014): 910–922, https://doi.org/10.1177 /0146167214529799.

13. Kristof, "Cure for Loneliness."

14. Brian Kennedy, Alec Tyson, and Cary Funk, "Americans' Trust in Scientists, Other Groups Declines," *Pew Research Center*, August 2, 2024, https://www.pewresearch.org/science/2022/02/15/americans-trust-in-scientists-other-groups-declines/.

15. Jessica Grose, "What Churches Offer That 'Nones' Still Long For," *New York Times*, June 28, 2023, https://www.nytimes.com/2023/06/28/opinion/religion-affiliation-community.html.

16. Grose, "What Churches Offer."

17. Sharon Brous, *The Amen Effect: Ancient Wisdom to Mend Our Broken Hearts and World* (New York: Penguin Random House, 2024).

18. Sharon Brous, "Train Yourself to Always Show Up," *New York Times*, January 19, 2024, https://www.nytimes.com/2024/01/19/opinion/religion-ancient-text-judaism.html?campaign_id=39&emc=edit_ty_20240119&instance_id=112926&nl=opinion-today&regi_id=74828348&segment_id=155752&te=1&user_id=b8c015625acf87b7c14d495e7b5f549e.

19. Brous, "Train Yourself."

20. Ariel Aberg-Riger, "'Solidarity, Not Charity': A Visual History of Mutual Aid," *Bloomberg*, December 22, 2020, https://www.bloomberg.com/news/features/2020-12-22/a-visual-history-of-mutual-aid.

21. *Mutual Aid 101*, Alexandria Ocasio Cortez Campaign, https://docs.google.com/document/d/e/2PACX-1vRMxVo9kdojzMdyOfapJUOB6Ko2_1iAfIm8ELeIgma21wIt5HoTqP1QXadFo1eZcoySrPW6VtU_veyp/pub.

22. Elizabeth Miller, "Mutual Aid Groups Rushed to the Rescue During COVID-19," *New Mexico In Depth*, September 28, 2020, https://nmindepth.com/2020/mutual-aid-groups-rushed-to-the-rescue-during-covid-19/.

CHAPTER FIVE

1. CeFaan Kim, "Angry Parents Rally Against Plan to Do Away With SHSAT Specialized Admissions Testing," *ABC News*, https://abc7ny.com/shsat-queens-testing-admissions/5244488/.

2. Frank Bruni, "The Most Important Thing I Teach My Students Isn't on the Syllabus," *New York Times*, April 20, 2024, https://www.nytimes.com/2024/04/20/opinion/students-humility-american-politics.html.

3. Bruni, "Most Important."

ENDNOTES

CHAPTER SIX

1. Travis Russell, "Budgets Are Moral Documents. Congress Should Treat Them Accordingly," *Jesuits*, September 27, 2021, https://www.jesuits.org /stories/budgets-are-moral-documents-congress-should-treat-them -accordingly/.
2. Elizabeth Dennis, "Women, Wealth and Investing—A Story of Evolution," *Morgan Stanley*, June 28, 2022, https://www.morganstanley.com/articles /female-invest-women-and-wealth; Pooneh Baghai, Olivia Howard, Lakshmi Prakash, and Jill Zucker, "Women as the Next Wave of Growth in U.S. Wealth Management," *McKinsey and Company*, July 29, 2020, https:// www.mckinsey.com/industries/financial-services/our-insights/women -as-the-next-wave-of-growth-in-us-wealth-management.
3. Loson-Ceballos and Layton, *In Abundance*, 42.

CHAPTER SEVEN

1. Victoria Colliver, "California Statewide Study Investigates Causes and Impacts of Homelessness," *University of California San Francisco*, June 20, 2023, https://www.ucsf.edu/news/2023/06/425646/california-statewide -study-investigates-causes-and-impacts-homelessness; Amy Graff, "The Most Surprising Findings in a New Study on Homelessness in California," *SFGATE*, June 20, 2023, https://www.sfgate.com/bayarea/article /california-homelessness-study-surprising-findings-18161475.php.
2. Another way to essentially start small if you're feeling overwhelmed is to cut yourself some slack by tapping into organizations that have already done the legwork. There are "collaborative funds" that aggregate dollars to support entire ecosystems of work. An example is the Groundswell Fund, which pools money from individuals and foundations and directs it toward reproductive rights and women of color–led organizing. The useful thing about these aggregators is that they do the work of finding great organizations working close to the ground, led by and for people most affected by the issue. I, as a reasonably well-informed person who cares about this issue, would have a hard time finding organizations in Kansas, Tennessee, or North Dakota, say—but if I give to this fund, they'll find them for me.
3. "Asian Women Giving Circle Awards $81,000 in Grants in 2023," Asian Women Giving Circle, accessed August 2, 2024, https:// asianwomengivingcircle.org/projects/.
4. Elena Acoba, "Lily Messing: Outstanding Youth in Philanthropy," *Tucson Lifestyle*, November 14, 2022, https://www.tucsonlifestyle.com/local/lily -messing-outstanding-youth-in-philanthropy/article_25cddab6-6469 -11ed-a431-07009acbb8a0.html.

5. Caitlin Schmidt, "Tucson Teen Philanthropy Group Gives $25,000 to Nonprofits—So Far," *Tucson.com*, February 19, 2023, https://tucson .com/news/solutions/tucson-teen-philanthropy-group-gives-25-000-to -nonprofits-so-far/article_661495 1c-910d-11ed-aebe-17fb1e487046.html.

6. D. W. Winnicott, *The Child, the Family, and the Outside World* (London: Penguin, 1973).

7. Marilyn Wedge, "What Is a 'Good Enough Mother'?," *Psychology Today*, May 3, 2016, https://www.psychologytoday.com/us/blog/suffer-the -children/201605/what-is-good-enough-mother; Charlotte Sidebotham, "Good Enough Is Good Enough!," *The British Journal of General Practice* 67, no. 660 (2017): 311, https://doi.org/10.3399/bjgp17X691409.

8. Lily Meyer, "What We Gain From a Good-Enough Life," review of *The Good-Enough Life*, by Avram Alpert, *The Atlantic*, August 18, 2022, https:// www.theatlantic.com/books/archive/2022/08/good-enough-life-winnicott -avram-alpert-book/671110/.

9. Meyer, "What We Gain."

CHAPTER EIGHT

1. Marvellina, "Indonesian Mie Goreng," What To Cook Today, June 25 2019, last modified November 25, 2020, https://whattocooktoday.com/indonesian -mie-goreng.html.

2. Loson-Ceballos and Layton, *In Abundance*.

3. There is an idea in feminism and other post-Marxist thought called "standpoint theory" or "standpoint epistemology." It posits that those who are marginalized in a community have a more complete and accurate view of society than those who are centered in the community—for example, people of color have a "better" view of social phenomena than white people. Standpoint theory argues that in order to survive, marginalized people must learn to see the world through their own eyes and also through the eyes of those who are centered, thus offering them a view that some authors compare to a baseball stadium, where the cheapest "worst" tickets are highest up and offer a view of the whole field.

4. From an interview in 2017.

5. Loson-Ceballos and Layton, *In Abundance*, 45.

6. "18% and Growing Campaign," Coalition for Asian American Children and Families, accessed August 2, 2024, https://www.cacf.org/policy -advocacy/budget-equity-18-and-growing-campaign.

7. Starsky Wilson, at Ignite conference, Palm Springs, December 2022.

8. Jennifer Velez, "BTS, Big Hit Entertainment and the BTS Army Donate Over $2 Million to Black Lives Matter," *Grammy Awards*, June 8, 2020, https://www.grammy.com/news/bts-big-hit-entertainment-and-bts -army-donate-over-2-million-black-lives-matter.

9. Barbara Ortutay, "TikTok Teens, K-Pop Fans Appear to Have Punked Trump's Tulsa Comeback Rally," CBC, June 22, 2020, https://www.cbc.ca /news/entertainment/trump-rally-tiktok-kpop-1.5621880.

10. One in an ARMY, "The Purple Effect: BTS ARMY Help Raise $1 Million through Independent Charity Fundraisers," *Medium*, April 25, 2020, https://oneinanarmy.medium.com/the-purple-effect-bts-army-help-raise -1-million-e87a646d8716.

CHAPTER NINE

1. Luke Jacobson, Ji Hoon Choi, Levi Herron, and Samantha Rich, "What Democratic Lawmakers Have Done With Their Trifecta in the First 100 Days," *Michigan Daily*, April 10, 2023, https://www.michigandaily.com /news/government/michigan-democratic-trifecta-100-days/.

2. Visit her author page here: "Melissa Walker," HarperCollins, accessed August 2, 2024, https://www.harpercollins.com/blogs/authors/melissa -walker-2015411640167.

3. "Our 2022 Stories of Impact Report," The States Project, accessed August 2, 2024, https://statesproject.org/2022-stories-of-impact/.

4. "The States Project," The States Project, accessed August 3, 2024, https:// statesproject.org/.

5. Community Investment Network conference, October 1–2, 2020.

· INDEX ·

I n 2021, Hali Lee was named to *Forbes'* "50 Over 50: Impact" in recognition of her work as a cofounder of the Donors of Color Network, the first-ever national network of wealthy folks of color; as a cocreator of Philanthropy Together, a national collective giving support organization; and as founder of the Asian Women Giving Circle. Her work has been covered by the *Washington Post, New York Times*, and *Good Housekeeping*, who called her "The Mindful Giver" and one of "10 Women Over 50 Who Prove It's Never Too Late to Change the World." Hali was born in Seoul, South Korea, and grew up in Kansas City. She lives in Brooklyn, New York, in the company of her family, a big love of a dog, an old cat, and rooftop honeybees.